Empowered By

GRACE

When the Impossible Becomes Possible

By

Dr. Dennis Burke

Empowered By Grace
When the Impossible Becomes Possible
ISBN 978-1-890026-23-3
© 2015 by Dennis Burke Publications
P.O. Box 150043
Arlington, TX 76015

Published by Dennis Burke Publications
P.O. Box 150043
Arlington, TX 76015

Text Design: Lisa Simpson

CONTENTS

1

YOUR MISSION, SHOULD YOU CHOOSE TO ACCEPT IT...

He will also go before Him in the spirit and power of Elijah...to make ready a people prepared for the Lord.

Luke 1:17

"The spirit of Elijah is on the Church." When the Lord spoke those words to me a few years ago, they rang out in my heart like a wake-up call. I knew instantly what they meant and the prospect of it thrilled me.

Having seen in the Old Testament the world-shaking power God poured out through Elijah, I had some idea of what could happen if God poured that same kind of power again. So to hear Him say with crystal clarity that He was already doing it sent spiritual shock-waves through me. It filled me with awe and permanently changed my perspective to think that the spirit of Elijah is on the Church right now.

Clearly, these are days when the spirit of Elijah is needed.

The evidence of it abounds. All over the world, the tide of spiritual darkness is rising. People are floundering. Individuals, cultures, even entire nations are losing their moral bearings. False religions and ruthless demonic ideologies are on the march. Christianity is coming under fierce attack from all sides.

In other words, what's happening on the earth right now could easily be compared to what was happening during Elijah's lifetime.

He lived in a day when evil appeared to have taken over everything. Even the Israelites, his own countrymen—God's set apart people—had been swallowed up by it. Under the leadership of their wicked king, Ahab, they'd completely turned away from the Lord. They'd forsaken His Covenant, forgotten His promises, and fallen into idolatry. Except for a small remnant, the entire population of Israel had slipped so deeply into deception they were actually worshipping the demon god named Baal.

Talk about some heavy spiritual darkness! Elijah faced it at a level most of us can't even imagine. And right in midst of it, God presented him with mission impossible. He called Elijah to turn the situation around.

From a strictly natural perspective, it couldn't be done. But because of the anointing that was upon him and his faith in the power of God, Elijah accepted the assignment. He gathered all the Israelites together and called for two altars to be built—one for Baal and one for Jehovah. Then he issued a challenge.

You call on the name of your gods, and
I will call on the name of the LORD; and
the God who answers by fire, He is God. So
all the people answered and said, It is well
spoken. (1 Kings 18:24)

If you've read the story, you probably remember what happened next.

Baal's prophets spent the whole day trying to
call down fire on their sacrificial altar. They did
everything they could think of to do: They cried
out, "Baal, hear us!" They leaped around. They
even cut themselves. But despite their frantic
efforts, nothing happened. They couldn't produce
a single, supernatural spark.

Then Elijah took his turn. Having exposed
Baal as a powerless imposter, he stepped up to
God's altar, doused it with water to make the
challenge more difficult, and prayed:

Hear me, O LORD, hear me, that this
people may know that You are the LORD
God, and that You have turned their
hearts back to You again. Then the fire
of the LORD fell and consumed the burnt
sacrifice, and the wood and the stones and
the dust, and it licked up the water that
was in the trench. Now when all the people
saw it, they fell on their faces; and they
said, The LORD, He is God! The LORD,
He is God! (1 Kings 18:37-39)

Don't you love it? With one awesome display of
God's power, Elijah decimated the demonic forces

that had deceived his nation. He put the enemies of the Almighty under his feet and turned the hearts of multitudes of people back to the Lord.

Now, in our day, the same kind of thing must happen again.

It must happen not only because the world is once again facing an onslaught of spiritual darkness, but because we're living at an appointed time in spiritual history. We're rapidly approaching the return of Jesus and certain things must be done before He comes. Just as John the Baptist prepared the way of the Lord at His first coming, now we, as the Body of Christ, are being called by God as Jesus' forerunners to fulfill the same assignment. To go before Him, as Luke 1:17 says:

> ...in the spirit and power of Elijah, 'to turn the hearts of the fathers to the children,' and the disobedient to the wisdom of the just, to make ready a people prepared for the Lord.

What exactly does it mean to "make ready a people prepared for the Lord"? The Greek word translated *make ready* describes a change that happens on the inside of people. It speaks of an operation of the Spirit that takes place inwardly, in their hearts. The word translated *prepare* refers to the outward, external results of that inward work.

This perfectly describes what the Holy Spirit is doing in and among us, as believers, right now. He's making us ready—both inwardly and outwardly—for Jesus' return. He's revealing to our spirits the fullness of what belongs to us in Him. He's supplying us with the grace, the divine inner substance we need to walk more effectively in His power in the last days of this age.

As this inner substance increases, what's happening on the inside of us will increasingly manifest on the outside and become more visible to the world around us. It will empower us to rise up in the anointing of God that we've heard about and believed was coming but haven't yet fully walked in. It will equip us to reign over the powers of darkness in Jesus' Name and show forth before the whole world the awesome might of our loving God.

In other words, the spirit of Elijah that's on the Church will prepare this planet for the second coming of the Lord.

UNRAVELING THE MYSTERY

This is, without a doubt, the most thrilling time in history to be a born again child of God. We're living in the day when Heaven and earth are coming together in a dispensation that will climax in an end-time spiritual explosion of light in the midst of darkness, the likes of which mankind has never seen.

We're actually experiencing firsthand the unfolding of the *mystery* referred to in the first chapter of Ephesians. There, unveiling the plan

God has ordained for us in Christ, the Apostle Paul wrote:

> In Him we have redemption through His blood, the forgiveness of sins, according to the riches of His grace which He made to abound toward us in all wisdom and prudence, having made known to us the mystery of His will, according to His good pleasure which He purposed in Himself, that in the dispensation of the fullness of the times He might gather together in one all things in Christ, both which are in heaven and which are on earth—in Him. (Ephesians 1:7-10)

Most of us, as believers, have read those verses for years without realizing what they're actually saying. We've sensed that they're important (with words like *mystery, dispensation,* and *the fullness of times,* they must be, right?), but we've breezed right through them and haven't stopped to consider what they mean. As a result, for the most part we've overlooked the stunning revelation they contain about the Church's ultimate calling and the great purpose God has for those of us who are growing up in Christ.

But we can't afford to overlook that revelation anymore. We've come to a point now where it's essential for us to understand it. Why? Because as those in the Church who have the privilege of preparing the way for the Lord's return, we're called to live it!

So let's take a closer look at what Paul said about this mystery. Let's think through this concept he presents about the grace of God abounding toward us for the purpose of gathering "together in one all things in Christ, both in heaven and on earth" (v. 10).

At first glance, such a gathering together seems like a contradiction. After all, in Heaven things always go God's way. Nothing is ever at odds with His will. Everything is done exactly as He likes it, so what happens there is always and only good. On earth, however, that hasn't been the case.

Things here generally have not gone the way God wanted. He didn't want sin to come in and kill people by separating them from Him. He didn't want disease, lack, failure, trouble, pain, and strife to mar the lives of all mankind. That wasn't God's plan. Yet it happened anyway. When Adam and Eve opened the door to the devil and his trash, all kinds of hellish havoc broke loose on this planet, and as a result, it's as different from Heaven as dark and daylight.

Why, then, does God want the two places to be brought together?

Because despite all that's gone wrong on earth, His will for it has always remained in exact harmony with what's happening in Heaven. In His mind, things could and should be done here just like they are there. What's more, according to Ephesians 1, His people are supposed to have the same mindset. As God's representatives on earth, we're called to be a part of manifesting His answer to the prayer Jesus prayed when He was here:

Your kingdom come. Your will be done
on earth as it is in heaven (Matthew 6:10).

We shouldn't just be looking forward to escaping the evils of this planet and enjoying a heavenly future someday in the sweet-by-and-by. We should have our hearts set on bringing Heaven's powers into manifestation in the rugged here and now.

I realize that's an astounding thought, given the fallen condition of the world around us. Yet it's exactly what God is preparing us, as the end-time Church, to do. He's maturing us inwardly so that outwardly, even while we're on this earth, we become reflections of Heaven. He's developing us in Christ so that in the midst of this present darkness, His power, life, and light can be revealed through us.

TIME IS TOO SHORT TO BE WASTED

"But Dennis," you might say, "I thought the gathering together of Heaven and earth is something that will happen at the second coming of Jesus. Didn't Paul say it will take place *in the dispensation of the fullness of time?*"

Yes, but that phrase doesn't refer to just one single moment. It refers to a period of time that includes days, months, and years.

You can see this is true by looking at Galatians 4:4. It says about Jesus that He was revealed as our Redeemer "when the fullness of the time was come." According to the Gospels, this revealing began with His birth, progressed throughout His life, and culminated in His death, resurrection, and ascension.

Jesus lived on earth for more than 33 years. The fullness of time during which His redemptive work unfolded spanned all of those years.

In much the same way, the fullness of time referred to in Ephesians 1:10 also spans a period of years. It began to unfold with the birth of the Church in Acts 2 and will culminate at Jesus' return. Often identified in the New Testament as "the last days," the fullness of time is the span of time we're living in right now.

The word *dispensation* is a powerful word. It refers to the stewardship or proper handling of something; the wise management or administration of a valuable resource that has been placed into your trust. You've heard the old saying, "Life is too short to be wasted." The same can be said about this last-days period of time we're living in. It's a valuable resource. It's too precious and it's passing too quickly to be squandered on things that are contrary to the will of God.

It's too short to be wasted on bitterness and strife.

It's too short to be thrown away on sin.

It's too short for us to let sickness steal it from us.

It's too short to be spent on anything less than God's great plan for our future.

As believers, we need to wisely steward the fullness of time!

One of the many passages in the Bible that provide us with insight into this stewardship is Psalm 110. It shows us a picture of God's end-time plan—both for the Church as a whole, and for us as individual believers. Although it's in the Old Testament, it speaks prophetically about the time in which we live and says:

> The LORD said to my Lord, "Sit at My right hand, till I make Your enemies Your footstool." The LORD shall send the rod of Your strength out of Zion. Rule in the midst of Your enemies! Your people shall be volunteers in the day of Your power... (vv. 1-3)

That is what's happening in our day! Jesus, having conquered His enemies—which include Satan himself and all his demonic hosts—is seated in Heaven and we, as His people, are learning to make His enemies His footstool. By His power and grace, we're growing up in Him and increasingly enforcing the victory He won through His death and resurrection. More and more, we're exercising His dominion over His enemies.

Although we, as believers, have always had the right and the potential to do this, up until now we haven't done it to the fullest degree. That's why in times past the devil retained somewhat of a hold on us. To some extent, we let him reign over us instead of us reigning over him. We stumbled over the obstacles he threw in our path and let him rob us of the total triumph that belongs to us in Christ.

But according to Psalm 110, that scenario is changing. As the fullness of time unfolds, the Church of the Lord Jesus Christ is rising up with increasing power and ruling over the devil and his works. We're putting every demonic strategy that has hindered us—every sin, every sickness, every fear that has harassed us—permanently and completely under our feet. We are becoming *volunteers in the day of His power.*

By definition, a *volunteer* is a person who offers to do something spontaneously. It's someone who gives themselves freely and willingly. When I picture a volunteer, I think of special operations soldiers, like the Navy Seals. When they have the opportunity to sign up for an important mission, they don't sit around thinking about it, wondering if they really want the assignment. They don't put off their decision and debate over it for a while.

No, they're Navy Seals! They live for such opportunities. The minute the commander asks who wants to go after the bad guys, they instantly volunteer. They don't even hesitate. They're eager to accept the challenge.

That's the kind of response we, as last days believers, have toward walking in the spirit of Elijah. We're eager to do it. When God says, "Who will walk in my power in this day? Who will bring into this age the power of the age to come?" something leaps inside us and we're ready to go. When He says, "Who will treat the devil like a footstool and reveal Heaven right here on earth?" we don't have to be talked into volunteering.

We instantly accept the challenge of bringing Heaven and earth together because we were born for this mission. We know deep in our spirit it's what God is calling us and gracing us to do. So we respond without a moment's hesitation.

Here am I, Lord! Send me! (Isaiah 6:8)

2

SONS OF THE LIGHT

Your people shall be volunteers in the day of Your power; in the beauties of holiness, from the womb of the morning...

Psalm 110:3

And He said to me, "My grace is sufficient for you, for My strength is made perfect in weakness." Therefore most gladly I will rather boast in my infirmities, that the power of Christ may rest upon me.

2 Corinthians 12:9

The mission you and I are taking on as God's last days volunteers is, much like Elijah's was, a mission impossible. The only way we can successfully carry it out is by the grace of God. So, in the coming days, we'll need to understand and operate in that grace more fully than ever before.

Discovering how to do that is what this book is all about. The revelations of grace we'll be exploring in the following chapters will help equip you to fulfill your part of God's plan in this crucial hour. They'll help you realize you really were born again for such a time as this. That God has actually chosen you to be a partaker of His grace at this particular point in history—not just so you can live a comfortable Christian life, but so you can help reveal His love and power to a sin-darkened world in the final crucial moments of this age.

You and I truly are living in the day of God's power. The return of Jesus is just ahead and we've stepped into the ultimate unfolding of what God promised through the prophet Joel in the Old Testament and the Apostle Peter in the New: "It shall come to pass in the last days, says God, that I will pour out of My Spirit on all flesh; and...I will show wonders in heaven above and signs in the earth beneath...before the coming of the great and awesome day of the LORD" (Acts 2:17-20).

Although you wouldn't guess it from watching the secular news, a worldwide move of God is already underway. Christianity is the fastest growing faith in the world by almost two to one over any other, and fired-up believers are having an impact on entire nations. I've seen evidence of it with my own eyes.

At a conference in Sweden a few years ago, I met ministers from all over Eastern and Western Europe. Every one of them was hungry for God to move mightily through them and turn their countries around. One group of ministers that came from Estonia had only been saved three or four years. They still felt very young in the things of God, yet they were already pastoring sizeable congregations and affecting a nation of several million people with the Gospel.

The same thing is happening in other parts of the world. In the Middle East, despite the violence of the terrorist groups, increasing numbers of Muslims are being saved. In China, it's said that nearly 25,000 people are being born again every day. Even under the continuing persecution and oppression of the Chinese government, the underground church is experiencing miraculous growth.

As wonderful as these things are, however, what's about to happen is greater still. It has to be. Before the coming of the Lord, the Gospel must be preached to the whole world (Matthew 24:14), and at the rate things are going now, even in China, where Christianity is spreading like wildfire, it will take over 100 years to reach the entire nation.

We don't have that much time left! So, clearly, God has a plan to increase the level of His anointing on us. He has a plan to pour out His presence and His power in greater measures upon and through the Church.

"But Dennis," you might say, "why would God pour out His power through me? I'm just a believer. I'm not a missionary. I can't influence the Muslim world or China or all those other faraway places."

Yes, you can. We can all have an impact on those places because the outpouring of God's Spirit has a collective effect. It flows from each one of us and becomes a river of divine power that pushes back the kingdom of darkness all over the world. You don't necessarily have to be in a particular location to bring Heaven's influence there. You can release that influence through prayer and through your faith. You can release it through your finances and by being involved in the work of God in other ways.

Don't ever underestimate your contribution as a believer. No matter who you are or where you might live, whatever you're called by God to do counts in a big way!

It counts in China. It counts in the Middle East. It counts in every nation on this planet because we're all part of this last-days move of God. As members of the Body of Christ, we're all called to show forth the greatness of God.

REFLECTIONS OF THE DAWN

One person who had a powerful revelation of this was the Apostle Peter. He witnessed, during the ministry of Jesus, an example of just how glorious those of us who are part of the Body of Christ can actually be. On the Mount of Transfiguration with James and John, he saw God's glory manifest through Jesus' physical body with such radiance that "His face shone like the sun, and His clothes became as white as the light" (Matthew 17:2).

It was a sight Peter never forgot. It so marked his thinking that many years later he referred to it in his second epistle. Writing to the believers of his day about how Jesus has "called us to receive his own glory" (2 Peter 1:3, NLT), he pointed back to the Transfiguration and said:

> We did not follow cunningly devised fables when we made known to you the power and coming of our Lord Jesus Christ, but were eyewitnesses of His majesty. For He received from God the Father honor and glory when such a voice came to Him from the Excellent Glory: "This is My beloved Son, in whom I am well pleased." And we heard this voice which came from heaven when we were with Him on the holy mountain. And so we have the prophetic word confirmed, which you do well to heed as a light that shines in a dark place, until the day dawns and the morning star rises in your hearts... (vv. 16-19)

Don't you love the imagery Peter used in those verses? It confirms what we've already seen in other passages of Scripture—that, both in the world and in our lives as believers, the glorious day of God's power unfolds gradually. It progresses toward its culmination over a period of time.

It comes like the dawn.

If you've ever gotten up in the early hours of the morning, you know how dawn comes. It doesn't arrive in a single flash. It slips in over the course of many minutes. Little by little, the night fades, and in the eastern sky, as a kind of forerunner to the sun, the morning star appears.

The morning star, of course, is actually the planet Venus. It isn't a star at all. Although it's the brightest light in the early morning sky, as a planet it doesn't generate its own light. It simply reflects the dawning light of the new day.

That's a perfect picture of us as believers. We're like the morning star. We don't generate our own light or power. We don't struggle along doing good things by our own efforts and try to keep a Christian smile on our face. As forerunners of the day of the Lord that's beginning to dawn, we simply reflect—from the inside out—the radiance of our God.

To do this, of course, we must be in proper relationship to Him. We must be positioned to catch His light, just as Venus is positioned to catch the light of the rising sun. That's the reason it's important for us to "take heed," as Peter said, to what God said in His Word. We need to know what He has planned for us in this hour. We need to stay alert to "the times and seasons" (1 Thessalonians 5:1) so we can receive the grace to walk out every aspect of our destiny in these last days.

Otherwise, we'll miss out on that destiny. Although we'll still go to Heaven when our life on earth is over, we won't experience everything God has planned for us on the way. I don't want that to happen to me, do you? I don't want to be spiritually asleep so that the day of the Lord comes on me "as a thief in the night" (v. 2). I want to be one of the "sons of light and sons of the day" (v. 5).

To me, the phrase "sons of light and sons of the day" sounds a lot like the reference to the morning star in Second Peter. It reminds us that in this hour, as the day of the Lord is dawning, we must stay in right relationship with the Son so we can reflect the right light!

A LITTLE IMPROVEMENT OR A GLORIOUS TRANSFORMATION?

To avoid any misunderstanding, let me make one thing clear: I don't claim to know how long it will be before Jesus comes back. I don't know exactly when the day of His return will break on the horizon of this sleeping, sin-darkened world. I just know we're in the dawning of it right now. We're living, at this very moment, in the slice of time Isaiah prophesied about in the Old Testament as he looked through the prophetic eye God gave him and said:

Arise, shine; For your light has come! And the glory of the LORD is risen upon you. For behold, the darkness shall cover the earth, and deep darkness the people; but the LORD will arise over you, and His glory will be seen upon you. The Gentiles shall come to your light, and kings to the brightness of your rising. (Isaiah 60:1-3)

Talk about reporting news before it happens! Those verses describe exactly what's going on in our day. This is a time of great contrast. On one hand, the light of Jesus is arising with ever greater brilliance upon His people. On the other hand, a great darkness is engulfing those in the world who aren't in relationship with Him. According to Isaiah, in the midst of this darkness, as the Church continues to grow brighter, sinners will be increasingly drawn to its light. They'll find their way to God because of the powerful way He's being revealed through believers.

I like how Hebrews 2:10 describes this. It says that, through Jesus, God is "bringing many sons unto glory." He's not just bringing many sons to Heaven—although we are going to Heaven and it will be wonderful—He's bringing us as His sons and daughters to the place where we embody Him on earth just as Jesus Himself did.

This is our destiny as members of the Body of Christ! But, by and large, we haven't caught sight of it yet.

As a result, we've lived far below where we belong. We've settled for self-help philosophies and limped through life, trying in our own strength to improve ourselves. All the while, God has provided something much greater for us. He's made His own power available to us to transform our soul into His own likeness, and take us "from glory to glory, just as by the Spirit of the Lord" (2 Corinthians 3:18).

Isaiah not only described this glorious transformation in Isaiah 60, in chapter 61 he told us how God would open the door to it. Prophesying about the coming of Jesus and the power and presence of God that would be released through His ministry, he said:

> The Spirit of the Lord GOD is upon Me, because the LORD has anointed Me to preach good tidings to the poor; He has sent Me to heal the brokenhearted, to proclaim liberty to the captives, and the opening of the prison to those who are bound; to proclaim the acceptable year of the LORD, and the day of vengeance of our God; to comfort all who mourn, to console those who mourn in Zion, to give them beauty for ashes, the oil of joy for mourning, the garment of praise for the spirit of heaviness; that they may be called trees of righteousness, the planting of the LORD, that He may be glorified. (vv. 1-3)

During Jesus' earthly ministry, He actually preached from this passage in Isaiah in his hometown of Nazareth. Using it as the text of His message, He read the first part of it and then announced, "Today this Scripture is fulfilled in your hearing" (Luke 4:21). He left out the verses about the day of vengeance of our God. But according to Isaiah, the day of God's vengeance is coming. In fact, it's unfolding right now.

Don't let that make you nervous, though. God's idea of vengeance is different from people's idea of it. People—because they generally tend to be ugly and hateful toward those who mistreat them—think of vengeance as harmful. They think it means, "You're going to get it now! I'm finally going to make you sorry you did me wrong!"

But that's not God's perspective, particularly when it comes to us as His born again children. For us, His vengeance is not bad news. It's Good News. It's our heavenly Father saying to us: "I will avenge all the things that have troubled you. I will avenge all the heartache that has wounded you. I will avenge all the fear and heaviness that has oppressed you."

That's part of His plan for us in this fullness of time!

RECEIVING HIS GRACE AND SHOWING HIS GLORY

"Well," somebody might say, "all this sounds wonderful, but I have to be honest. If I'm going to reveal God's power the way you're talking about, something will have to change in me. I'll need more divine power manifesting in my life than I've had in the past."

Me too. But that's okay, because such power is available. The first chapter of John assures us of it. Referring, as Peter did, to the glory of God that was on Jesus on the Mount of Transfiguration, it says:

> The Word became flesh and dwelt among us, and we beheld His glory, the glory as of the only begotten of the Father,

full of grace and truth…And of His fullness we have all received, and grace for grace. For the law was given through Moses, but grace and truth came through Jesus Christ. (vv. 14, 16-17)

Notice in those verses, John didn't just say we *beheld* Jesus' glory. He also said we've *received* of Jesus' fullness (which, of course, includes His glory). Then he explained what makes this receiving possible. It's the grace of God! "For the law was given through Moses, but grace and truth came through Jesus Christ."

Think about that statement for a moment. It uses the words *grace* and *truth* to distinguish what Jesus makes available to us from what the law of Moses made available. But let me ask you something: Wasn't the law that came through Moses truth?

It was, wasn't it? It came from God, so it had to be truth. Yet the truth of the law alone wasn't enough to make people free from their sin. Although it made temporary atonement for their sins through sacrifices and offerings, it didn't redeem them and cleanse them from sin on the inside. Therefore, even though people who were under the law walked in elements of truth, they didn't have the freedom of truth. They couldn't fully live the truth because what Moses brought them didn't supply them with the power to do so.

What Jesus brought, however, was different. Although He came as the Truth, He brought more than truth. He also brought grace.

What is grace?

Grace is the empowering to do the truth! It's God's divine influence on our hearts and the reflection of that influence in our lives. It's His active power at work in us enabling us to do His will.

Certainly, grace includes the favor of God that moves Him to give to us freely because of His love and not on the basis of our performance, but it's more than that. It's also the supernatural ability that makes it possible for us to reveal through our lives in a tangible way the real peace, the real power, and the real presence of God. It's the divine strength that enables us to do what, in our own strength, we could never do.

In the time we have left before Jesus returns, as we help prepare this planet for His coming, we must clearly walk in greater measures of this divine strength than we have in the past. We must learn how to receive, as never before, "grace upon grace" (John 1:16, NASB).

As we do, even though the world may grow darker around us, we can shine like the morning star, brighter and brighter. We can be *in* the world but not *of* it. We can be transformed from glory to glory, as more and more by the working of God's Spirit and His amazing grace, His Word is made flesh in us.

3

I CAN'T...BUT HE CAN

So all the work that Solomon had done for the house of the LORD was finished; and... indeed it came to pass, when the trumpeters and singers were as one, to make one sound to be heard in praising and thanking the LORD...that the house, the house of the LORD, was filled with a cloud, so that the priests could not continue ministering because of the cloud; for the glory of the LORD filled the house of God.

2 Chronicles 5:1, 13-14

To get a sense of the magnitude of the power God wants to pour out through the Church in our day, imagine for a moment the cloud of God's glory. Imagine what you might experience if it rolled into the room where you're sitting right now the same way it once rolled into Solomon's Temple. Picture it shimmering all around you with the light of God, enveloping you so completely in the atmosphere of Heaven that, like the priests in Second Chronicles, you could hardly move.

What do you think could happen in the presence of that kind of divine power? What miracles could be wrought? What needs could be met? What changes could take place?

Now, think about this: God's grace is what empowers you and me, as believers, to press into that kind of glory.

It's astounding to consider, isn't it?

But it's the absolute truth.

"How can I be sure of that?" you might wonder. "How can I really be certain it's God's will to manifest Himself today like He did back then?"

Because the Bible says God doesn't change (Malachi 3:6). And He's always wanted to pour out His power and His presence upon His people. It's a part of His nature, of who He is and what He does. As Psalm 84:11 says:

> The LORD God is a sun and shield; the LORD will give grace and glory...

The phrase "the Lord will give grace and glory" is a scriptural promise. It belongs to you and me today just as surely as it did to the Israelites in the Old Testament. In fact, it belongs to us to an even greater extent than it did to them, because God's glory and His grace are connected, and according to the New Testament:

- We've been saved *by grace* (Ephesians 2:5).

- We live in *the dispensation of God's grace* (Ephesians 3:2).

- And throughout *the ages to come* God intends to show toward us *the exceeding riches of His grace...* (Ephesians 2:7).

In other words, as New Covenant believers, we're grace people! God is in the business of showing off His grace in and through us in every possible way; not only for our own benefit but for the benefit of others. He wants them to be drawn to Him by the grace they see upon us.

How can people *see* grace?

In a literal sense, they can't because grace is a spiritual force. It's invisible to the natural eye. When we steward it wisely, however, it produces visible results. It not only works within us, it causes God's glory to flow through us, and that glory is what people see.

I'm not saying they'll necessarily see it in the form of a thick cloud like the one described in Second Chronicles. They probably won't. God's glory doesn't usually manifest through individuals in such a spectacular and dramatic way. But it will manifest through each one of us in other ways that are just as real and supernatural, because that's God's desire. He wants to do things in every believer's life to demonstrate His power and His goodness; to express who He is and what He can do.

The Lord spoke this to me years ago, and it's been growing in me for decades: Before Jesus catches away the Church, we'll see the most awesome manifestations of God's divine power and presence that have ever been seen. We'll experience the greatest move of God in human history. We'll learn to walk in God's grace until we're transformed into the Church Jesus is coming to receive as His bride: "a glorious church, not having spot, or wrinkle, or any such thing; ... holy and without blemish" (Ephesians 5:27).

GOD'S EMPOWERMENT CHANGES EVERYTHING

So, let's take an even closer look at what grace actually is. Let's dig around a little more in what the Bible says about it.

In both the Old and the New Testaments, the word *grace* is often connected with what the *Amplified Bible* calls "God's unmerited favor" or His loving kindness that brings blessing and prosperity into a person's life, not because they've earned it, but as a gift which God in His goodness freely gives.

For most Christians this is the most familiar aspect of grace, and it's absolutely wonderful. I can personally say I'll be forever grateful for it. I definitely need the undeserved favor of God in my life and have plenty of stories to prove it. I won't share them here because it wouldn't edify anybody. But suffice it to say, I've learned from hard experience I could never qualify for God's grace on the basis of my own merit.

None of us can.

Many people try, of course. They think if they just do more, maybe God will move in their life. They think if they just read enough scriptures and pray enough prayers, if they go to church enough, maybe He'll fix their problems. As a result, they wear themselves out on a religious treadmill of self-effort and condemnation.

God doesn't want anyone to get caught on that treadmill. He's said to everybody, "Jesus has already qualified you to receive all My favor and My blessings. Just put your faith in Him and receive them."

For it is by free grace (God's unmerited favor) that you are saved (delivered from judgment and made partakers of Christ's salvation) through [your] faith. And this [salvation] is not of yourselves [of your own doing, it came not through your own striving], but it is the gift of God. (Ephesians 2:8, AMP)

Truth be told, if this were the only aspect of grace, we could all spend eternity praising God for it because it's so amazing and marvelous. But that's not the only aspect of it. As I've already mentioned, grace also refers to God's divine influence in our inner man, and the reflection of that influence coming out in our lives.

This influence is immeasurably powerful and valuable. It supplies us with direction for our lives. It gives us ideas. It enables us to hear and understand that which we previously haven't heard or understood. It provides us with supernatural strength to do the will of God.

In more ways than I can even begin to name, the divine influence of God's grace empowers us to accomplish what we could never accomplish on our own.

Why is such empowerment important? Because, as you've probably noticed, God has a tendency to give all of us commands we don't feel qualified, capable, or strong enough to carry out. Although He's well aware of our natural limitations and inabilities, He frequently seems to be totally unimpressed by them. Knowing what we cannot do, He tells us to do it anyway.

"But Lord," we say, "You don't understand. I CAN'T DO THAT!"

"I know it," He answers, "but this isn't about your ability, it's about Mine. It's about My power working in and through you."

When God's power comes on the scene, it changes everything. It turns *No way!* into *Yes, Lord, okay. Let's do it!*

I've seen it happen in my own life countless times. One instance in particular stands out in my mind. It was back in 1981. I'd been teaching for months on the subject of meditating God's Word, and the Lord started talking to me about putting what I'd been teaching into a book.

The thought of me writing a book seemed so preposterous I thought surely He was kidding. "Lord," I said, "do you remember what I was doing during my high school English classes? I certainly don't! I was totally zoned out when Mr. Gilbert was teaching us about things like nouns, verbs, and adverbs. The only book I read in my entire high school career was *The Old Man and the Sea*, and I only read that one because I had to write a book report and it was the shortest book I could find. I'm not sure I'm the right person for this job."

Ignoring my arguments, the Holy Spirit persisted. "I want you to write the book," He said.

It wasn't a suggestion. Although the tone was gentle and loving, it was a command. So instead of just saying no, which would have been disobedient, I tried to negotiate. "Lord, I know people who are really good at writing. I'll be happy to talk with them about this and get them to do it for You."

When the Lord didn't go for that idea, I decided to get another opinion. I talked to my wife about it. "Vikki, what would you think if I kind of...sort of...considered the possibility of starting the process of writing something...that might ultimately end up being a book?"

"I believe that's the will of the Lord," she said. "And I believe you need to get started on it right now."

It was not what I wanted to hear. But, like God, my wife doesn't buy my excuses. So after consulting her, I had double trouble. Now I not only had the Holy Spirit after me, Vikki was after me, too.

"Have you started that book yet?"

"No, Vikki, I haven't."

"Well, you need to get on it."

Would you just leave me alone and let me be disobedient in peace? I thought (but did not say, because I value my life).

After a number of such conversations, I finally surrendered. I said, "All right, Lord. I'll write the book. But if I'm going to write it, somebody will have to read it. And for anybody to read it, a publisher will have to publish it. There's no way I can make that happen, so it's completely up to You."

Apparently, the Lord was up to the challenge. Within a couple of weeks, I unexpectedly bumped into Buddy Harrison of Harrison House publishing. We'd barely exchanged greetings when I found myself blurting out the unthinkable. "The Lord told me to write a book on meditating the Word and I'd like Harrison House to publish it." To my amazement, he said, "Okay," and asked when I could have it written.

"Next month," I said.

Next month?

Yes, that's what I said. I don't know what I was thinking. I guess I figured it would take a miracle for me to write the book at all and I didn't want to drag the process out for a year. So I just said, "Come on, Jesus, let's get it done!"

My schedule for the following three weeks was already full, which meant I only had one week that month I could spend writing. So when that week arrived, I sat down at the kitchen table with my notes and books, and prayed a very deep prayer. "Lord, if You love me, You'll have to do something here!"

You can probably identify with the feeling. We all have times in our lives when we need something supernatural to take place. Something we can't generate ourselves. That's the situation I was facing. I was not going to be able to come up with a book on my own. It could only happen by the power of God.

Sure enough, it did.

For the next four days, I spent six hours a day writing at the kitchen table. By the end of the fourth day, I'd finished the manuscript. I gave it to Vikki, she made English out of it, and Harrison House published it.

Today, the book continues to be a valuable ministry tool that blesses people. Although I've written other books since then, I'm still amazed when I remember how that one came to be. I know very well it only exists because of God's empowering grace.

GOD ISN'T WRINGING HIS HANDS

"Well, the Lord hasn't asked me to write a book," you might say. "Do I still need this empowering aspect of His grace?"

Yes, you do. Hebrews 12:28 makes that crystal clear. It says to all of us, "Let us have grace, by which we may serve God acceptably with reverence and godly fear." The word translated *acceptably* means according to God's ability. It refers to what we do, not by our natural talent or determination alone, but in the strength of the Lord.

The things we can accomplish only by God's empowering grace are what truly bring honor to Him. But, as most of us would have to admit, those are often the things we'd rather avoid. We prefer to operate within the parameters of what we can do rather than what we're pretty well certain we cannot do. So when God calls us to the latter, we have a tendency to try to argue with Him.

As I've already acknowledged, I know this firsthand. I've argued with the Lord on any number of occasions, so I can tell you from personal experience it's a waste of time. No matter how much we whine about how incapable we are, God won't change His mind about what He's called us to do.

If you need proof of it, read about Moses. When God called him to be His voice to Pharaoh and the nation of Israel, and deliver the Hebrew people out of Egyptian slavery, Moses felt totally unqualified. He told God flat out that he couldn't do it—not because he had an inferiority complex, but because from a natural perspective he truly wasn't up to the task.

> O Lord, I am not eloquent or a man of words, he protested. I am slow of speech and have a heavy and awkward tongue... Oh, my Lord, I pray You, send by the hand of [some other]. (Exodus 4:10, AMP)

From Moses' viewpoint this seemed like a rational argument, but it didn't impress God. He didn't change Moses' calling and go looking for a more silver-tongued orator. He stuck with His original plan. In His mercy, He did make one concession, though: He gave Moses permission to let his brother Aaron be his spokesman. "He shall speak for you to the people, acting as a mouthpiece for you, and you shall be as God to him" (v. 16).

It must have sounded like the ideal solution. Who wouldn't enjoy telling his brother what to say and being treated like God? That would surely be satisfying. Yet the Bible doesn't indicate Moses ever took advantage of that opportunity. Instead of asking Aaron to do the talking, he stepped up and did it himself because when God spoke to him, His words burned in Moses' heart like a fire. They got so big inside him he couldn't hold them back.

God's empowering grace will do the same kind of thing in our lives. It will work within us and supply us with everything we need to fulfill our divine calling, just as it did for Moses. That's why God isn't sitting on His throne wringing His hands and worrying about our natural limitations. It's why He doesn't buy our arguments and redesign His plans for us so that they'll fit within the framework of our meager human abilities.

He's already made available to us more than enough power to get the job done! He's given "to each one of us grace...according to the measure of Christ's gift" (Ephesians 4:7).

I know what you're probably thinking right now. If God has already given us such a boundless measure of grace, why is it we still struggle sometimes?

Because we need to increase and develop in that grace to become all God designed us to be, and most of us haven't made that a goal in our lives. We haven't purposely set out to "grow...in grace," as Second Peter 2:18 says, because we haven't really understood how much depends on it.

Exactly how much does depend on it?

Pretty much everything that matters, according to the Apostle Paul. He wrote again and again in his epistles that his entire life and ministry depended on God's grace. He said, anything of value he'd ever done was only because "the grace of our Lord was exceedingly abundant [toward me]" (1 Timothy 1:14).

In First Corinthians 15:10, he put it this way: "By the grace of God I am what I am..."

Some people might consider that statement surprising. Given Paul's natural abilities, he appeared to be quite capable of achieving success on his own. After all, he did possess a great, natural intellect and an advanced education. Even today, he's still considered by secular scholars to have been one of the world's most brilliant men. A few years ago, a major news magazine devoted an entire issue to him. Recounting his accomplishments and how he helped shape the modern day civilization, *Time* named him one of the ten greatest minds in recorded history.

Yet Paul knew his intellectual capacity wasn't the key to his success. His education and his natural talent weren't what caused God's power to manifest so miraculously in his life. His power came from the inner substance God gives to every believer—the supernatural substance of divine grace.

The Lord said to Paul, "My grace is sufficient for you, for My strength is made perfect in weakness" (2 Corinthians 12:9), and he never forgot it. He believed in that grace and grew in it until he could say at the end of his life: "I have fought the good fight, I have finished the race, I have kept the faith" (2 Timothy 4:7).

You and I can do the same. Although we haven't been called to accomplish exactly what Paul did, each one of us in our own unique way can manifest more and more of God's power, presence, and love as we grow...and grow...and grow in God's exceedingly abundant grace.

4

GETTING RID
OF THE RESISTORS

*For those who were once enlightened,
and have tasted the heavenly gift...have
become partakers of the Holy Spirit, and
have tasted the good word of God and the
powers of the age to come...*

Hebrews 6:4-5

The devil doesn't fight believers very hard over the idea that someday, way off in the future, we're going to show forth God's glory. He doesn't get especially upset when we say that eventually, after we get to Heaven, we're going to partake of what Hebrews 6:5 calls "the powers of the age to come." But when we start believing that, by grace, we can bring the power and glory of the age to come into this age we're living in right now, the devil reacts with a vengeance.

The reason is simple. He knows all too well what that power can do.

He's seen it in operation. He saw it eons ago in Heaven, where it flows freely with nothing to resist it and produces God's perfect will. He saw it 2,000 years ago on earth, when it flowed unhindered through Jesus, and destroyed his evil works (1 John 3:8).

The devil understands that he can't afford to sit idly by now, while we learn to walk in increasing measures of that kind of power and further devastate his kingdom. So he fights us over it, tooth and toenail. He opposes us at every turn and tries to stop us from operating in it.

One way he does this is by filling our lives with things that limit the amount of God's power that can manifest through us. I refer to such things as *resistors,* because they have much the same effect on us spiritually that natural resistors have when they're put on an electrical circuit to regulate the amount of power that goes to a machine.

Although I'm no expert electrician, I've learned as I've worked with my own equipment over the years what electrical resistors can do. If they put too much resistance on the circuit a machine is plugged into, the machine won't run. It just sits there—not because there's anything wrong with it, but because it's being starved of power.

You can tear the machine apart, thinking, *What in the world is the matter with this thing? I've got it plugged in. It doesn't appear to be broken. It should be running fine!* You can press all the buttons. You can pull every lever. But you're not going to get the problem fixed until you remove the resistors.

The same principle holds true for us as believers. There's nothing wrong with our spirit. We've been born again and recreated on the inside in the image of God. We've been plugged into Jesus and, through the Holy Spirit, the powers of the age to come have been made available to us. So if those powers aren't flowing freely through us, it's often because they're being hindered by resistors of some kind.

Sin, for example, is a resistor. Unforgiveness is a resistor. Unbelief, worldliness, wrong priorities—all those things are resistors that restrict the flow of God's anointing and manifested presence in our lives.

Sadly, however, many people in the Body of Christ don't realize this. So they attribute their spiritual powerlessness to other factors. They talk themselves into believing, for instance, that the power of the age to come simply isn't meant for them. They wish it was; they're hungry for it; but since they're not experiencing it, they conclude it's just not God's will for them to walk in it. They decide He must intend for it to operate only in the lives of special people, like the apostles.

This might seem like a reasonable theory. But there's one problem with it. Jesus' teachings contradict it. He said, in Matthew 7, there are only two roads in life: the "broad...road that leads to destruction" and the "narrow...road that leads to life" (vv. 13-14, NIV). He didn't mention anything about a mysterious third path.

Christians who theorize their powerlessness is God's will, however, seem to think they've found one. They know they can't be on the path of destruction. "Certainly not!" they say. "I love the Lord. I go to church and believe in Jesus. I'm headed for Heaven." But then they don't think they're on the narrow road, either—the road where the power is. "I guess I must be on the road that's for regular Christians," they say, "the road that's for believers who just go to work every day and live an ordinary life."

Is there really any such road?

Not according to Jesus. He made it quite clear there are only two—the wide and the narrow. The reason there seems to be a third alternative is because many Christians get on the narrow road, and instead of moving forward, they just park. As a result, there's actually a wide portion on the narrow path. There's a place where Christians who aren't progressing, crowd together in one big spiritual parking lot.

Personally, I don't want to live in a parking lot of any kind. I'm sure you don't either. And thank the Lord, we don't have to. Anytime we choose, we can get our lives in gear and move full speed ahead on the road that leads to ever greater power and more abundant life.

But to do it, we must start getting rid of the resistors.

STIR UP THE FIRE AND GET FREE

"How do you go about doing that?" you might wonder.

According to Second Timothy 1:6, one thing you can do is "stir up the gift of God which is in you."

The phrase *to stir up* speaks of rekindling a fire or fanning a flame. The word *gift* comes from the Greek word *charisma*, a derivative of *charis*, the word for *grace*. Put together, they indicate that, although God has already kindled on the inside of you as a believer the gift of his fiery power, you have to do what's necessary to keep it hot. If you don't, the devil will use the things of the world to tamp down that inner fire and cool it off.

D.L. Moody used to warn: "Anything that cools you off toward God is worldly."

Anything. It doesn't matter what it is. It might be something that's outright sin, or it might be something that seems relatively harmless, like a hobby or a career that becomes such a priority it edges God out of the top spot in your life. It might even be church work that keeps you so busy you don't have time to fellowship with the Lord and spend time in His Word.

"Really? Church work can actually be worldly?"

Yes, it can, if it cools you off toward God.

I've known of full-time ministers who proved this. They got so achievement-minded doing the work of God they all but lost sight of the Lord Himself. They went to Bible school, learned how to preach and do church business, but they never took time to fellowship with Jesus much at all. So although they made a decent living, had a fine medical plan, and retired comfortably, they never stepped into the wonderful plan God had for their lives.

Any of us as believers can fall into that trap. We can learn how to be an accepted part of religious society. We can be proud of the fact that we don't smoke, we don't chew, and we don't run with those who do. Yet if we don't stir up the *charisma* gift God has deposited on the inside of us, instead of really living, we'll end up just surviving.

If we do stir up that gift, however, we'll have marvelous experiences. We'll live the overflowing, victorious life God has planned for us. Nothing the devil does will be able to stop us, because anything that might restrict the flow of God's power in our lives will be conquered and consumed by the white-hot fire of His grace.

Seriously. God's grace—His *charisma*—is that powerful.

It isn't like the natural version of charisma the world has. It's not just a superficial ability to charm people. It doesn't just bring empty popularity. God's charisma contains His supernatural ability. It empowers us to do what, on our own, we could never do...including obey the command in Hebrews 12:1: "Let us lay aside every weight, and the sin which so easily ensnares us."

"I don't know about that, Dennis," somebody might say, "I've been trying to lay aside tobacco for years and I haven't been able to do it. I know the Lord wants me to but there's just too much about it I enjoy. I like the smell. I like all the gadgets that go with it. I have a whole collection of cool ashtrays and lighters I like to flick. I like everything about it."

"At the same time, though, I also hate it. I have to buy mints by the case and sprays to cover up the smell; and I feel condemned every time I light up. I love the Lord and don't want to disobey Him, yet I just can't seem to quit."

I understand. I've had to deal with a few habits like that myself. I didn't smoke as long as some people have, but back when I was a teenager, before I was born again, I smoked anything that would burn. I took trips into the cosmos without ever leaving the house and thought it was fun. I also hacked and coughed every morning for the first five minutes of the day, but I was too hooked on getting high to care.

I'm not proud of this, and it's in the distant past now, but I bring it up to make a point: Everybody has had weights and sins to deal with in their lives. We've all had things that, in our own strength, we couldn't lay aside. For some people it might have been tobacco, for others it might have been alcohol, pornography, worry, gossip, or carrying grudges.

So don't feel condemned and down on yourself about the resistors you happen to be struggling with. But then, don't let the devil continue to use them to stop the power of God from flowing freely in your life, either. Instead, call on Jesus for help.

Nobody understands better than He does how desperately we, as human beings, need God's grace. He needed it Himself when He was on earth. Luke 2:52 confirms this. It says that as a young man, "Jesus increased in wisdom and stature, and in favor…" The word *favor* is the Greek word *charis,* or grace.

Think of it! Even as the sinless Son of God, Jesus had to grow in grace in order to manifest His Father's glory. So He knows that for us to bring the Father's glory into the world like He did, we're going to need grace, too. And He doesn't require us to clean ourselves up in order to qualify for it. He says, "Come to Me as you are. I won't reject you. I'm on your side. I'll help you get free. I'll show you how good life can be by teaching you to access God's grace."

To get the picture of what it means to access God's grace, switch mental gears from spiritual things to natural for a moment and think of your computer (or your iPad, or smart phone, or whatever). It's full of wonderful information, but you have to access that information for it to benefit you. It doesn't just leap out at you because you need it. You have to tap into it by giving the computer the correct command.

That's easy enough for you to do because, most likely, you understand how your computer operates. But if you didn't, you'd be in trouble. You could end up filling your computer screen with error messages and making no progress. Even with the information right there at your fingertips, available to you in abundance, you could find yourself unable to utilize it because you don't know how to work with your computer's operating system.

As believers, we can find ourselves in a similar situation if we don't know how to access God's grace. We can have it available to us in limitless abundance but be unable to benefit from it. So to make sure that doesn't happen, we want to learn everything we can about God's operating system.

And Jesus is the One who can teach us.

WATCH AND PRAY,
LEST YOU ENTER INTO TEMPTATION

In Matthew 26, He provided us with one of the all-time greatest examples about how to tap into God's grace. There, in one of the most sobering passages of the New Testament, we find Him facing not only the darkest moment in His own life, but the darkest moment in all of human history. He was just a few hours away from going to the cross. Staggered by the prospect of it, He'd gone with Peter, James, and John to the Garden of Gethsemane where He became sorrowful and deeply distressed.

> Then He said to them, "My soul is exceedingly sorrowful, even to death. Stay here and watch with Me." He went a little farther and fell on His face, and prayed, saying, "O My Father, if it is possible, let this cup pass from Me; nevertheless, not as I will, but as You will." Then He came to the disciples and found them sleeping, and said to Peter, "What? Could you not watch with Me one hour? Watch and pray, lest you enter into temptation. The spirit indeed is willing, but the flesh is weak." Again, a second time, He went away and prayed, saying, "O My Father, if this cup cannot pass away from Me unless I drink it, Your will be done." And He came and found them asleep again, for their eyes were heavy. So He left them, went away again, and prayed the third time, saying the same words. (vv. 38-44)

It's important to understand as you read these verses that Jesus wasn't exaggerating when He said His soul was exceedingly sorrowful, even unto death. He was speaking the literal truth. The sin, grief, and oppression of all mankind had begun to press in on Him, and the stress of it was about to kill Him. He was in danger of dying right there in Gethsemane, before He could even get to the cross.

To make matters worse, His human nature was drawing back from what was about to be required of Him. Though He wanted in His heart to fulfill His divine mission, His flesh didn't want to be crucified any more than yours or mine would. In His humanity, He didn't want to go through with it.

That's why He said, "If it is possible, let this cup pass from Me, Nevertheless not as I will but as You will." His will wasn't in alignment with God's.

For some people this is a shocking concept. They've been told that if they don't want what God wants every moment of every day, they're in sin. That if they're really walking with the Lord, they'll always want to do what He commands. But as nice as that might sound, real life doesn't always play out that way.

In my life, for instance, when God told me to write that first book, my flesh drew back from it, and though that was a very small thing compared to what Jesus went through, it put me through a personal crisis. At times, I've also struggled with the will of the Lord in other areas. When He asked me to put a larger amount in the offering than I intended, for instance, or He told me to give away something I considered valuable or precious, I sometimes wanted to say, "Father, please don't ask me to give that thing away. I want to keep it!"

I'm sure you've had similar experiences. All believers have, because no matter how much we love the Lord, our will doesn't always immediately line up with His. But that's not sin. It only becomes sin when we disobey God and do things our own way.

Jesus had never done that, not even once. Although He was tempted just as we are, throughout His life He'd always overcome temptation. And in Gethsemane, as He faced the ultimate challenge of going to the cross, He was determined to overcome it again. Regardless of how He felt, He was committed to acting not on His own will, but on the will of God.

So what did He do? He honestly faced His own weakness. He looked at what was lacking in Himself and, unwilling to allow that lack to remain, He went to the one place where He could obtain what He needed to triumph over the fleshly resistance and satanic darkness that was coming against Him. He went to God's throne of grace.

How did He get there?

Through prayer.

He prayed—once, twice, three times—not prayers of dominion or of seemingly great power, but prayers of commitment that revealed real human weakness. And through those prayers He accessed the grace of God that empowered Him to overcome.

His disciples, who were there with Him in Gethsemane, could have done the same. In fact, He urged them to do so, saying, "Watch and pray, lest you enter into temptation." But they didn't heed His warning. Peter, in particular, soon regretted it. Before sunrise the next morning, he denied Jesus and ended up weeping bitter tears.

Every one of us can identify with Peter's experience to one degree or another. We've all noticed in ourselves a tendency to sin first, and then cry about it later. "Oh, God, I'm so sorry!" we say. "I feel so bad! Oh, Jesus, I wish I hadn't done that! I repent!"

It's good to repent when we sin, and God is always faithful to forgive us. But think how much better it would be if we prayed and cried out to God for grace *before* we did anything we needed to repent of. That's what Jesus did. When He was tempted to draw back from going to the cross, before that temptation got the best of Him, "He...offered up prayers and supplications, with vehement cries and tears to Him who was able to save Him" (Hebrews 5:7). He kept praying until He'd accessed the empowering grace He needed to carry out God's will.

Once He obtained that grace, He got up from His place of prayer ready to complete His mission. Awakening His drowsy disciples, He said, "Are you still sleeping and resting? Behold, the hour is at hand, and the Son of Man is being betrayed into the hands of sinners. Rise, let us be going. See, My betrayer is at hand" (vv. 45-46).

Then Judas, having received a detachment of troops, and officers from the chief priests and Pharisees, came there with lanterns, torches, and weapons. Jesus therefore, knowing all things that would come upon Him, went forward and said to them, "Whom are you seeking?" They answered Him, "Jesus of Nazareth." Jesus said to them, "I am He."...Now when He said to them, "I am He," they drew back and fell to the ground...Then the detachment of troops and the captain and the officers of the Jews arrested Jesus and bound Him. (John 18:3-6, 12)

No question about it, that was a stunning turnaround.

Suddenly, instead of being sorrowful, stressed, weak, and weighted down, Jesus was so full of God's power that when He spoke to the soldiers who came to arrest Him, His words knocked them flat on their back. They didn't fall down praising the Lord, either. This wasn't a Pentecostal church service! Those soldiers came with murder on their mind. Yet they were so overcome by the presence of God they wound up on the ground staring up at the stars.

The fact that Jesus waited for them to get up and arrest Him reveals He was in total control of what was happening. No one was telling Him what to do. No one was taking His life from Him. He was obeying the Father and walking out the plan of God. He was laying His life down of His own free will.

He wouldn't even say anything in His own defense when He went before the High Priest and Pilate that night. He kept His mouth shut because if He'd spoken up on His own behalf He would have been delivered. The power of God would have hit, and nobody would have been able to get up off the floor, much less condemn Him to be crucified.

"Don't you realize that I could ask my Father for thousands of angels…and he would send them instantly?" He said at one point. "But if I did, how would the Scriptures be fulfilled that describe what must happen now?" (Matthew 26:53-54, NLT).

THE POWER THAT STANDS UP
TO ANYTHING HELL HAS TO OFFER

Just think about what God's grace did for Jesus in this situation! When He walked out of Gethsemane, He was very different from the way He was when He went in.

When He went in, He was facing trouble, just like you may be facing trouble. He felt overwhelmed, just as you may feel overwhelmed at times. He thought the pressure He was under was going to kill him, just as you may think sometimes that the pressure you're under might kill you.

When He went in, He was humanly unable to do what He was being called by God to do. He was facing a demonic assault that was more than His flesh could stand. But during those hours in Gethsemane, He tapped into the divine empowerment that can stand up to anything Hell has to offer, and He walked out as a conqueror. He came out calm and full of divine power, because He'd been to the throne of God's grace.

Today, that same throne of grace is available to you and me. And because of what Jesus has done for us, we can approach it with the same confidence He did.

As Hebrews 4:15-16 says:

> For we do not have a High Priest who cannot sympathize with our weaknesses, but was in all points tempted as we are, yet without sin. Let us therefore come boldly to the throne of grace, that we may obtain mercy and find grace to help in time of need.

This is what the early Apostles discovered. They found out that through prayer they could access more and more of God's all-powerful grace. They discovered they could continually pray for an increase of God's grace not only in their own lives but in the lives of the believers in the churches of their day. That's why in the New Testament epistles they wrote again and again, "Grace and peace be multiplied to you" (2 Peter 1:2).

Multiplied grace is a wonderful thing! It unlocks in us, as believers, what we cannot generate by ourselves. It releases within us the substance of God's supernatural power, so that when we're facing the worst moments of our lives we'll have what we need—not just to put up with the situation or barely make it through, but to come out in victory, just as Jesus did.

"But Dennis," you might say, "Jesus isn't like me! He didn't have to deal with the same kinds of resistors I do."

Yes, He did! He dealt with those resistors, not only by facing and overcoming all the same temptations we do, He dealt with them by becoming sin for our sake. As Second Corinthians 5:21 says, "God made him who had no sin to be sin for us, so that in him we might become the righteousness of God" (NIV).

Notice, according to that verse, Jesus didn't just pay the price for sin and leave it in place. By taking it upon Himself and dying on the cross, He destroyed sin's hold on us. He "subdued, overcame, and deprived it of its power over all who accept that sacrifice" (Romans 8:3, AMP). He broke the back of the kingdom of darkness and every resistor the devil ever devised—and He did it all by the grace of God.

Now, the power of that grace is inside of you and me!

That means when we come to God's throne, and He points out the resistors the devil has slipped into our lives, we don't have to panic. We can just repent and have confidence in Jesus, who takes up our cause and says to God, "Heavenly Father, You know I paid the price for those resistors to be removed from their life. So now they have a right to be freed from them."

Because Jesus has already conquered sin's power once-and-for-all, we don't have to run away from God when we sin, feeling condemned and unworthy, thinking we have too many problems and failures to ever receive anything from Him. We can march right into His presence and stay there until we've dealt with the sins and weights that have been sapping us of spiritual power. We can reach out to Him in faith and obtain the grace we need to get rid of them.

"Can they really be gotten rid of that quickly?"

Certainly they can. If the nature of sin can be changed in a heartbeat when a person prays to receive Jesus as Lord; if a person can been born again and delivered out of the dominion of darkness and into the kingdom of God in a moment of time; then resistors, too, can be wiped out in an instant by God's grace.

The problem is when people are struggling with resistors, most of the time they won't get honest with the Lord about them. They won't acknowledge the sin in their lives, take it to Him, and receive the grace to deal with it. So the flow of His power in and through them continues to be limited.

But it doesn't have to be that way for you. You can take the limits off!

You can come into God's presence where His grace is imparted. Even at times when it feels like your whole world is caving in and falling apart; even when you feel like you've utterly failed; you can come with boldness to the throne of grace. You can worship the Lord and sing to Him. You can pray and fellowship with Him, and He'll reframe your perspective. He'll remind you of His Word and help you see things from His point of view.

That will cause your faith to flourish. And as you respond to Him according to faith, He'll respond to you according to His grace. He'll make the impossible possible for you. He'll strengthen you with His might until the threats of the devil don't threaten you at all.

He'll empower you to throw off every sin and the weights that have dragged you down so that, just like Jesus, you can walk out of your place of prayer into a whole new realm of glory.

5

THE LIBERATING
LAWS OF GRACE

*You therefore, beloved...grow in the grace
and knowledge of our Lord and Savior
Jesus Christ. To Him be the glory both now
and forever. Amen.*

2 Peter 3:17-18

Since God's grace is what empowers us to get
free from the resistors in our lives and reveal
more of His power and presence to the world
around us, as believers, we want to continually
grow in that grace. But to do so, we must be able
to answer the question, what exactly does it mean
to grow?

According to the dictionary, the word *grow*
has two different meanings. On one hand, it can
refer to an increase in size or amount. As we've
already seen, in the area of grace we experience that kind of growth by praying. We access
increased amounts of God's grace by going to His
throne and receiving it.

On the other hand, growth can also refer to
advancement. It can speak of developing skill and
maturity; of gaining wisdom and understanding.

For us to flourish the way God intends in any area of life, we must have both of these kinds of growth. If we don't, we won't flourish like we should. We'll fall short of what God has planned for our lives.

I found this out on a scholastic level many years ago in high school Algebra. The skill I developed in that class definitely fell short of what everybody had planned. The reason was simple. Although I showed up for class every day and was exposed to vast amounts of information, I failed to understand the mathematical principles upon which Algebra is founded.

I don't know why I struggled with those principles so much. I guess the idea of mixing numbers with letters like x and y just never seemed right to me. I found it especially offensive that the values of those letters kept changing. I'd work on one equation and think, *I've finally figured out what* x *is!* Then I'd go to work on another equation and find out I was wrong.

I'm happy to report that later in life I eventually caught on, but while I was in high school, my algebraic skills never advanced very much. So my growth remained stunted in that area for years.

I share this bit of personal history because it illustrates what can happen to us as believers in the area of God's grace. We can be exposed to lots of information about it. We can find out that it belongs to us and read in the Bible that we've been given "the abundance of grace...through the One, Jesus Christ" (Romans 5:16). But if we don't grasp the basic principles necessary to develop in that grace, we won't grow up in it. We'll wind up like the immature Christians described in Hebrews 5:13, crawling through life as "unskilled in the word of righteousness" as "a babe."

There's nothing wrong with babies, of course. They're adorable. Everybody loves them. But they're also a bundle of needs. That's why we're all grateful that children aren't designed to remain babies forever. They're supposed to grow, both physically and developmentally. They're supposed to start learning how to do things and taking on some responsibilities.

If they progress properly, eventually they become adults who not only take care of themselves but are a blessing to others. That's what real maturity is all about. But such maturity doesn't come automatically. As many people have proven, it's possible to grow old physically without ever really growing up into real adulthood.

By the same token, it's also possible for us, as believers, to be saved for years and never mature spiritually. We don't grow up in the Lord just because time is passing. We don't grow up just because we go to church every Sunday for 50 years. We grow up when we start making choices that move us out of the stage of infancy where life is all about our needs.

"Dennis, are you saying we should mature to the point where we don't talk to God about our needs anymore?"

Of course not. We'll always look to God to meet our needs. He'll always be our Daddy and we'll always be His children, regardless of how spiritually mature we become. The Bible assures us of this. It never refers to us as God's "adults." Instead, it consistently addresses us, in one way or another, as His "little children" (1 John 3:18) because we are and always will be completely dependent on Him.

We should also notice, however, that nowhere in the Scriptures does God call us His "little babies." Although He's well aware that we're born again as spiritual infants, He expects us to immediately begin growing and developing. He expects us to start right away becoming real disciples.

What's involved in becoming a disciple? Among other things, it involves taking personal responsibility for our own spiritual development. We become disciples when we realize that how much we grow up in grace is up to us. It's not up to the pastor, or the prophets, apostles, evangelists, and teachers God has put in our lives. Although those people can certainly help our growth along by providing a beneficial spiritual environment for us, bringing forth truths from the Word of God and encouraging our faith, they can't make us spiritually mature.

We're the only ones who can do that. We're the only ones who can make the choices and take the actions that cause actual growth to occur in our lives. Nobody else can do it for us—not even the Lord Himself. He won't do our believing for us. He won't do our praying for us. He won't do our giving for us.

That's not how He designed things to work. He set up His Kingdom so we can be actively involved in the operations of it. He designed us to grow up spiritually and take responsibility for doing our part to bring forth results.

If we don't do our part, we'll become frustrated and exasperated. We won't experience the fulfillment of the promises He's made to us in His Word. Instead, those promises will remain continually in the distance. Rather than becoming a manifested reality in our lives, they'll start to seem almost like fairy tales...all because we're waiting for God to do what He has commissioned us to do ourselves.

NOT A LEGALISTIC SET OF RULES
BUT A SUPERNATURAL OPERATING SYSTEM

One thing God has commissioned us to do that many believers have overlooked is this: He wants us to discover and learn how to cooperate with the supernatural systems He's put in place. He wants us to activate and benefit from His spiritual laws.

"Laws?!" you might say. "I thought God only gave laws in the Old Testament. We're New Testament people!"

Indeed we are. Yet in Hebrews 10:16-17, God said this about us:

> This is the covenant that I will make with them after those days, says the LORD: I will put My laws into their hearts, and in their minds I will write them...Their sins and their lawless deeds I will remember no more.

Those words first appeared in the Old Testament, but they're quoted in Hebrews because they refer to what God has done for us through Jesus. They tell us that under the New Covenant God isn't remembering our sins anymore, or bringing up the bad things we've done in our past. He's forgiven us, freed us from condemnation about our fleshly failures, and empowered us to live based on what Jesus has done rather than what we can do ourselves.

Those are clearly New Testament truths. Yet God connects them in this passage of Scripture with "laws." What laws? The ones He wrote on our hearts when we were born again.

I have to confess I never gave those laws a lot of thought until a few years ago. I simply assumed they were similar to the standards of morality God gave the Israelites through Moses in the Old Testament. I figured that God took rules like the Ten Commandments, wrapped them all together and put them on the inside of us so we wouldn't have to live just by what's written down somewhere; we could know on the inside what's right and what's wrong.

One day as I was studying these verses, however, I realized there had to be more to it. The laws God has put within us as believers couldn't possibly be just an internal set of moral standards. Everybody has those—even people who aren't born again. Whole societies throughout history that were never taught the Ten Commandments have understood that things like murder and stealing and lying were wrong. They didn't have to be told. It was just built into them.

So, in Hebrews 10, God must have had something else in mind. He must have been talking about laws that would bring His kingdom alive within us and produce the evidence of it in our experience. He must have been referring to a kind of law that would liberate, empower us, and radically change the way we live.

The laws God gave through Moses never did that. They just provided rules for people to follow. They declared what was legal and what was illegal in various situations, and decreed what punishments were to be meted out to lawbreakers. Much like the laws our government makes today, the laws of Moses were the kind of laws that imposed regulations on every area of life.

To be clear, I'm not suggesting those laws were bad. They weren't. They brought truth to people.

They let them know: if you do these things you'll die. They even made it possible for people to receive some mercy through a system of sacrifices and offerings. Even so, however, Old Testament laws didn't liberate or empower anyone. They did the exact opposite. As the Apostle Paul explained in his letter to the Corinthians, the Mosaic laws actually became a "ministry of death, written and engraved on stones," and a "ministry of condemnation" (2 Corinthians 3:7, 9).

Now obviously, if God is going to write something on the hearts of His New Testament children, it's not going to be the ministry of death and condemnation. Certainly not! Through Jesus, we've been delivered from death. We've been brought out of condemnation. We've been given the free gift of righteousness and God's abundant grace. Therefore the laws referred to in Hebrews 10 must fall into an entirely different category than the Old Testament laws. They can't be about just following rules and regulations. They must be another kind of law.

What kind are they?

They're laws that pertain to the operation of certain systems. They're laws that reveal how those systems work and make it possible for us to benefit from them.

In the natural realm, there are many such laws. There are laws of mathematics, for example (which, if I'd understood them, would have helped me succeed in high school Algebra).

There are laws of Physics that, properly applied, can produce wonderful results. There are laws of Chemistry that make it possible to either combine the wrong chemicals in the wrong proportions and accidentally blow up the science lab, or combine the right chemicals in the right proportions and create something great.

The spiritual laws God has written in our heart are much like those natural laws. They're operational principles that help us benefit from His spiritual systems. The more we understand and apply them, the more we can grow and develop in grace. So let's take a look at four of them the New Testament specifically mentions.

THE LAW OF FAITH

The first law I want to highlight is found in the third chapter of Romans. There, the Apostle Paul, referring to the righteousness of God and the grace that comes upon all who believe in Jesus, said this: "Where is boasting then? It is excluded. By what law? Of works? No, but by the law of faith" (v. 27).

Look again at that last sentence. It describes faith as a law—a law of grace.

That almost sounds like a paradox, doesn't it? We usually think of law and grace as being at odds with each other—and in some ways they are. As we've already established, we can't qualify for God's grace by keeping rules and doing good deeds. On the contrary, trying to earn God's grace through legalistic endeavors will keep us from receiving it. Therefore regulatory laws and grace oppose each other.

But the law of faith isn't a regulatory law. It isn't legalistic. Faith is a God-designed, God-ordained system. It's the method by which we gain "access...into this grace in which we stand" (Romans 5:2). It's the system by which we live. Hebrews 10:38 leaves no question about this. It says clearly, "Now the just shall live by faith."

No wonder God has written the law of faith inside the heart of every believer! He put it within us so we could use it. He gave it to us so that we could put it to work for our own benefit and the benefit of others, just like Jesus did during His earthly life and ministry.

Jesus operated by faith all the time. We can see evidence of it throughout the Gospels. In Mark 11, for instance, Jesus used faith to deal with a rebellious fig tree. When it left Him hungry and lied to Him by putting out leaves that made it look fruitful when it actually had no fruit on it at all, Jesus answered it with words of faith. He said, "Let no one eat fruit from you ever again" (Mark 11:14).

Sure enough, no one ever did. By the next day that fig tree was graveyard dead, withered up from the roots. When Jesus and His disciples passed by and saw it, the astonished disciples exclaimed over its quick demise, and Jesus responded by saying to them:

> Have faith in God. For assuredly, I say to you, whoever says to this mountain, "Be removed and be cast into the sea," and does not doubt in his heart, but believes that those things he says will be done, he will have whatever he says. Therefore I say to you, whatever things you ask when you pray, believe that you receive them, and you will have them. (vv. 22-24)

I know what you might be thinking: *Get real, Dennis. Surely you don't really believe God will literally move mountains just because we talk to them by faith?*

Yes, actually I do. But I also believe that the mountains we need to move in our lives tend to be more metaphorical than literal. Rather than being made up of rock, dirt, and trees, they're usually composed of circumstances and problems that prevent us from progressing in God's plan for our lives.

Regardless of what kinds of mountains might be standing in our way, though, what Jesus said remains true: We can remove them by living in a manner that puts the power of faith to work on our behalf. We can operate the law of faith the way God designed and talk to the obstacles we encounter like Jesus talked to the fig tree. And we can get results just like He did.

To do so, however, we must go beyond just believing that God exists. We must believe what He said in His Word, act on it, and grow in our understanding of the law of faith.

THE LAW OF THE SPIRIT OF LIFE

A second operational law of grace is *the law of the Spirit of life in Christ Jesus*. It's mentioned in Romans 8:1-2:

> There is therefore now no condemnation to those who are in Christ Jesus, who do not walk according to the flesh, but according to the Spirit. For the law of the Spirit of life in Christ Jesus has made me free from the law of sin and death.

The word translated *life* in those verses comes from the Greek word *zoe*. It's the same word Jesus used in John 14:6 where He said, "I am the way, the truth, and the life."

This *zoe* kind of life is what came into our spirit when we were born again. It's the supernatural, divine life that God Himself has, and it's a system we can learn to live by. It's an operating law God has imprinted in our hearts.

The benefits we can experience by cooperating with the law of the Spirit of life are marvelous and varied. They affect us in every way—not just spiritually, or in the area of our soul, but physically too. If our body is attacked by sickness, for instance, the Spirit of life can drive it out. We don't have to wait for God to send healing to us. He's already infused us with His healing power by putting within us the law of His *zoe* life. By activating that law with our faith we can receive healing anytime we need it.

Another benefit of the law of the Spirit of life is that it continually provides us with divine guidance. It functions as a kind of supernatural GPS, or God-positioning system, by locking in on our destiny in Christ and helping us stay on course. When we're heading the right overall direction, the Spirit of life within us gives us a sense of peace and well-being. It confirms in our hearts that we're on the right track.

That's a tremendous blessing! Spiritually, just as in the natural, it's a great comfort to know you're on the road that takes you where you want to go. You don't have to be concerned about making wrong turns. You can just keep moving ahead, enjoying the journey, confident you'll eventually reach your desired destination.

If for some reason, as you're traveling toward your destiny, you do happen to take a detour, or make a turn that starts to take you in the wrong direction, the Spirit of life will alert you to the problem. Your sense of peace and inner buoyancy will recede. Things will start to seem kind of life-less and flat on the inside of you. Then you can seek the Lord about it, make the necessary corrections, and get back on the right track.

In my life, I depend on such guidance every day. In ministry, for example, I'm frequently presented with invitations from people I don't know very well, asking me to minister in places I've never been. So I look to the Holy Spirit for direction. I ask Him, *Is this a place I need to go? Is this something I should be involved with?*

I don't mean to infer there's anything wrong with any of the invitations I receive. The people who ask me to minister are godly and precious, and sharing the Gospel with anyone anywhere is always a good thing. So when I'm endeavoring to discern which invitations I should accept, rightness or wrongness is not the issue.

Actually, for us as believers, rightness and wrongness should never be the issue. That's the way of thinking that got Adam and Eve in trouble in the Garden of Eden. They ate from the Tree of the Knowledge of Good and Evil because they wanted to live according to a system of right and wrong. But that wasn't God's plan for them. He wanted them to eat from the Tree of Life so that they'd have the Spirit of life and be guided by God Himself.

He wants the same for us as His children today.

For me, that means if I get an invitation to go to Pakistan and minister at a big conference, I don't have to think about the rightness or wrongness of it. I simply seek to know what God is directing me to do. I ask the Lord, is it His plan for me to go or not? Then I check my heart and, without fail, the law of the Spirit of life on the inside of me gives me the answer.

This is how all of us as believers are designed to live. It's an essential part of growing in grace and every Christian has the capacity to do it. We can all follow the leadership of the Spirit of life because it's one of the laws God has written in our hearts.

This doesn't mean, of course, we'll be able to perfectly discern the Lord's leadings the instant we're born again. It usually takes some time for us to get familiar with them. We have to develop confidence in our ability to cooperate with the law of the Spirit of life and that comes by experience.

So if you're just getting started, you might want to practice on little things. Instead of waiting for life and death issues to come up, check your heart for the Lord's direction as you plan your daily schedule. Ask Him to guide you while you're at work, or at the grocery store. As you go about your normal routine, ask Him to lead you to someone who needs a word of encouragement; then look to Him to show you what to say.

Ordinary days can become an adventure when you're living by the law of the Spirit of life!

THE LAW OF LIBERTY

Another grace law that can turn your life into an adventure is what the New Testament refers to as *the law of liberty*. According to James 1:25:

He who looks into the perfect law of liberty and continues in it, and is not a forgetful hearer but a doer of the work, this one will be blessed in what he does.

This law, although it overlaps the other grace laws and works together with them, specifically deals with anything that would try to keep you in bondage. It releases you from the captivity produced by strongholds of sin and weaknesses of the flesh. It sets you free from fears that would try to plague and paralyze you.

The law of liberty declares that because of what Jesus has done through His death and resurrection, liberty rules and reigns within you. You don't have to live anymore in the shadow of the bad things people did to you when you were a kid. You don't have to remain boxed in by the limitations that once defined you. You've don't have to continue to receive the negative things that have been passed down to you through your family tree.

The divine decree has been made. It's been engraved on the inside of you. Those works of the devil no longer have any right to dominate your life. You can drive them out. God has given you the grace. Whether or not you use that liberating grace, however, is up to you. If you want to experience all the blessings God has provided for you, you must choose freedom.

The Apostle Paul said, "It is for freedom that Christ has set us free. Stand firm, then, and do not let yourselves be burdened again by a yoke of slavery" (Galatians 5:1, NIV). So keep growing in grace. Live by the law of liberty.

6

THE ROYAL LAW OF LOVE

...and from Jesus Christ, the faithful witness, the firstborn from the dead, and the ruler over the kings of the earth. To Him who loved us and washed us from our sins in His own blood, and has made us kings and priests to His God and Father, to Him be glory and dominion forever and ever. Amen.

Revelation 1:5-6

I don't know if you think of yourself as royalty, but as a born again believer you absolutely are. You're a child of Almighty God and a member of His Royal Family. You're a joint-heir with the King of Kings, and according to the Bible, He's made you a king, too. Which means the last law of grace we're going to discuss is especially relevant to you.

It's referred to in James 2:8 as "the *royal law* according to the Scripture," and it's the governing principle behind the spiritual system God designed. It's also the law He has commanded us as His regal sons and daughters to live by. Repeated again and again throughout the New Testament, it's both supremely powerful and so simple any child can remember it.

"You shall love your neighbor as yourself."

Although that's hardly a new or complicated concept, most people (including many believers) don't fully understand what it means. They don't realize that the love it refers to is a very specific kind of love. The Greek word for it is *agape*. A word that was rarely used until the time of Jesus' ministry, it speaks of divine love: the kind of love that God has.

His love is totally different from natural human love. Human beings put conditions on their love. They say, "I love you," but what they really mean is, "I will love you as long as you qualify for it." Of course, they don't usually admit this, even to themselves. But somewhere in the back of their mind they're thinking, *If you don't look at me right, you won't get my love. If you don't do what I want you to do, or you act unlovely, I won't love you. If you cross me and make me mad, I'll make you pay.*

That's not the way God loves. He doesn't require people to qualify for His love. He gives it freely and unconditionally. He loves everyone, no matter how undeserving they might be.

As believers, we're called to do the same. In our relationships with other people, we're to "be imitators of God as dear children, and walk in love, as Christ also has loved us" (Ephesians 5:1-2).

Most Christians I know are actually quite eager to do this. We're all very hungry to give to others the God-kind of love. There's just one problem: In our own human strength we can't. It's impossible. In ourselves, we don't have that kind of love. Since we can't give to others what we don't have, the first thing we must do is go to God and receive from Him what we're lacking.

As First John 4:19 says, "We love each other as a result of his loving us first" (NLT). So we can only love as God loves when we've settled the core issue that we ourselves are loved by Him.

How do we get that issue settled?

We put our faith in what the Bible says about it. We believe, for instance, what's written in John 17 where Jesus prayed for us, as believers, and said to the Father:

> The glory which You gave Me I have given them, that they may be one just as We are one: I in them, and You in Me; that they may be made perfect in one, and that the world may know that You have sent Me, and have loved them as You have loved Me...I have declared to them Your name, and will declare it, that the love with which You loved Me may be in them, and I in them. (John 17:22-23, 26)

Talk about faith building words! Those verses tell us that our heavenly Father loves all of His children with the same love He has for His First-born Son. That there's no difference between the love God has for Jesus and the love He has for us.

For most of us, such a thought almost defies comprehension.

It's no stretch for us to grasp the idea that God loves Jesus. After all, He and the Father are one. There's no separation, friction, or struggle between them, so there's nothing to get in the way of their great love for each other. But to think we're included in that union and are recipients of the same love? That's something else altogether!

To believe that, we must dismiss all the reasons we think we're not worthy of such love. We must set aside all the ugly things we know about ourselves and receive God's *agape* by faith, trusting that anything in our lives that might have hindered or interrupted it was dealt with by Jesus when He went to the cross.

Sadly, many Christians never take this step of faith. Although they love the Lord, they spend their entire lives being uncertain about His love for them. As a result, they're unable to live a truly victorious life. They can see in the Bible such a life is available, but their faith to lay hold of it remains weak because they've never "believed the love that God has for us" as believers (1 John 4:16).

THE GREATEST HAPPINESS IN LIFE

Not long before I began writing this book, I sat at the bedside of such a woman. She was in the last stages of cancer. She'd struggled to receive healing for years and experienced some real miracles but, having gotten discouraged along the way, she'd surrendered the fight and had only a few days left to live. Vikki and I had been close to her for many years, so I knew she was born again and that her walk with the Lord had been less than she'd hoped.

Her life had been tough for a lot of different reasons. So as I took her fragile hand, I began to reaffirm to her the love and goodness of God. She listened for a while, and then in the midst of our conversation she asked me this question. "Do you think I'm going to Heaven?"

"Yes, I do," I answered. "I know you are, and I'll tell you why. I've heard you say that Jesus is your Lord and Savior. That's true, isn't it?"

"Yes, it is," she answered. "He is the Lord of my life."

"Well, the Bible says if we believe Jesus is Lord and we say so, we are saved. And one of the many benefits of being saved is Heaven becomes our eternal home."

"But Dennis, I've sinned!" she protested. "I've done some bad things. I've lied. I've stolen…"

Sensing she needed to unburden her heart, I tried to wait quietly for her to finish her long list of trespasses (most of which had been committed decades ago). But eventually, I interrupted her. "I know you did those things," I said, "but here's what you need to know: God isn't looking at any of them. He's washed them away in the blood of Jesus and He doesn't even remember them anymore.

"When He looks at you now, He sees you through the lens of the sacrificial offering made by His Son. He sees you as worthy of His best blessings. Because of what Jesus has done, God has forgiven you and He loves you! So just believe and receive that love. Let it saturate your thinking so that you're not tormented by these things anymore."

Over the years I've met many other believers who needed to hear those same words of comfort. Maybe, right now, you need to hear them, too. Maybe you're thoroughly saved and completely forgiven but still carrying the shame, blame, guilt and torment of past sins you've committed. You're wondering, *How could God love me, a sinner, who would do such bad things?*

I'll tell you how God could love you: the same way He loves all the rest of us who've ever done anything wrong.

In God's eyes, there are no levels of evil. There are no tiny sins or little white lies. To Him all sin is the same so, apart from Jesus, we're all equally guilty. But by the same token, once we receive Him, we're all equally righteous and perfectly loved!

> For there is no difference; for all have sinned and fall short of the glory of God, being justified freely by His grace through

the redemption that is in Christ Jesus. (Romans 3:22-24)

Knowing that God loves us is the foundation of our walk with Him. It's the only way we can really live by faith. Galatians 5:6 says faith works by love. So if we're going to believe for and receive all the blessings that Jesus purchased for us through His death and resurrection—which in addition to forgiveness from sin includes peace in our home, healing in our body, financial provision, and an abundance of other good things—we must not only embrace the fact that God has provided those things for us, we must realize He did it for only one reason: because He loves us as much as He loves Jesus Himself.

Sometimes I like to say it this way: God doesn't just *love* us; He's *in love* with us!

Clearly, there's a vast difference between those two. I can say from my own experience, for example, that on a very casual level I *love* Harley-Davidson motorcycles. I *love* hamburgers, and going on vacation, and a lot of other enjoyable but inconsequential things. On a much higher level, I also love people. Lots of them! But when it comes to being *in love*, it's a different story. I'm in love with one woman. Only one.

Her name is Vikki, and we've been running together for more than 40 years now. Hers is the voice that I recognize over any other voice. I could be in a crowded room and if she called my name I'd instantly know it was her, even if I didn't know she was there. My ears are tuned to her voice because I'm in love with her and she's in love with me—and that's a wonderful thing!

As good as it is, however, the love God has for us is even more perfect. He's not only in love with us, He *is* love, and we're the target of it. That's why He's always giving to us. It's why He sent Jesus. As John 3:16 says, "For God so loved the world that He gave His only begotten Son, that whoever believes in Him should not perish but have everlasting life."

God never changes. He still loves the world, and He's still giving. He's not a taker. He doesn't come into anybody's life in order to get something from them. He comes to give to all who will receive it, His absolute and unconditional love.

The great Christian author, Victor Hugo, once said, "The greatest happiness in life is the conviction that we are loved; loved for ourselves, or rather in spite of ourselves." God is the only Source of that kind of love. When we put our faith in Him and embrace the love He has for us, something shifts in us and we find happiness.

But that's not the end of the matter. Once we've received God's love we start wanting to give it to others so that they can experience that happiness too. We start loving people who don't deserve it. Instead of waiting for them to "qualify" for our love, we look at them and think, *Hey, God loves me without condition, so now I'm free to love you the same way. I don't have to base my love for you on what you've done or not done. I can love you out of the overflow of the love He has shown toward me.*

IT'S IMPOSSIBLE TO RIP OFF A GIVER

"But Dennis," you might say, "If I love without qualification, I'll just have to let people walk all over me. I'll wind up being everybody's doormat!"

No, you won't. Jesus is the ultimate example of God's love, and He certainly wasn't anybody's doormat when He was on earth. If you need proof of it, think about how He dealt with the religious leaders who falsely accused Him and tried to push Him around. He always held His ground against them. Although He didn't strike back at them, He refused to let them stop Him from doing what God had commissioned Him to do. At one point in His ministry He even said to them, "Your approval or disapproval means nothing to Me" (John 5:41, NLT).

Notice, He didn't say, "*You* mean nothing to Me." He didn't withhold His love from them. He just let them know He wasn't going to allow anything they said or did to change Him.

Jesus intends for us, as His disciples, to take the same stand.

"Well, then why did He teach us to turn the other cheek? Wasn't He saying that if people treat us wrong, we should just drop our guard and let them do it again?"

No. Jesus told us to turn the other cheek as a way of saying to people who come against us, "Nothing you do to me is going to penetrate who I am. Nothing you say is going to change me because I don't gain my victory in God, or my sense of well-being, by your approval or disapproval. I'm rooted in my heavenly Father's love. So regardless of how you treat me, I remain the same."

To be clear, I'm not implying we should necessarily say such things out loud, in the heat of the moment, when somebody is causing us trouble. Nor am I suggesting we should adopt an arrogant, I-don't-need-anybody kind of attitude that alienates us from other people. I'm just saying that God's love for us makes it possible for us to stop worrying about what other people are doing or not doing for us. It liberates us so we can love them on His level, without binding them to a list of obligations and expectations. Because God is freely giving to us, we're free to give unreservedly to them without worrying that they're going to rip us off in some way.

After all, we know God will take care of us in the end. Regardless of how anybody else may choose to treat us, He'll lead us, bless us, and see to it that our every need is met in abundance. As First John 4:18 says, "There is no fear in love; but perfect love casts out fear." So when we're secure in God's love for us, we can live fear-free lives. We don't have to be afraid that somebody will permanently damage us by withholding from us something we need or taking something away from us. This in itself will free us from a lot of the unloving tendencies we've had when interacting with others.

What kind of tendencies?

Outbursts of anger, for instance. They're almost always rooted in fear. When people lose their temper, it's generally because they're afraid someone is going to hurt them—emotionally, or financially, or whatever. Most people (especially if they're Christians) initially try to find a peaceful way to solve the problem. They ask the person who's upsetting them to change their behavior. But when the person doesn't respond in a satisfactory manner, they lose their temper and explode.

People who don't have explosive personalities may express their anger differently. They might take the passive-aggressive route and ignore the other person, giving them the silent treatment. They might resort to manipulation or intimidation. Whatever a person's tendency might be, however, those kinds of angry reactions are almost always rooted in fear. They erupt when somebody is afraid they're not going to be okay unless another person does what they want them to do.

Another unloving effect fear sometimes has on people is to make them shy and withdrawn. It stops them from reaching out to those around them. It keeps them self-focused, always worrying about what others might think or say about them.

On the opposite end of the spectrum, fear turns other types of personalities into control freaks. It makes them feel like they have to keep a tight grip on everything. As a result, they're always taking over conversations. They can't delegate tasks to others without demanding every detail be reported back to them. They deal with a heavy hand and insist things always be done their way. Such people think they're being strong, but in reality they're very weak. They're afraid of being out of control.

Because the love of God flushes fear out of our lives, it sets us free from these tendencies. It enables us to rest in the assurance that God has our back, so to speak. That He'll provide for and protect us in every situation. Although this doesn't mean things will always go just right and we'll never feel any pain, it does mean that whatever others around us might do, we can continue to love them because we know we'll ultimately be just fine.

I discovered this in a very personal way a number of years ago. I'd been struggling with some problems in my life and as I sought the Lord about them, He showed me they were a result of a nagging sense of insecurity I carried. I'd picked it up when I was 13 years old and my dad committed suicide. Although I'd never blamed myself for his death (or God, or even my dad, for that matter), his absence had left me feeling abandoned at some level.

When the Lord revealed this to me, I'd been in ministry for years. My life was fruitful, and I considered myself blessed. But I could see the gap that had been left by my father's suicide was still having a negative effect on me. When I asked the Lord what to do about it, He took me to Psalm 27:10. "When my father and my mother forsake me, then the LORD will take care of me." Or, as one translation puts it, "Even if my father and mother abandon me, the LORD will hold me close" (NLT).

When I read that verse and embraced it by faith, God set me free from the sense of abandonment I'd carried. He let me know that even when the most important people in our lives let us down, He will uphold us. He'll meet our needs in a way they never could. He'll heal the wounds that others have inflicted so that we suffer no permanent harm.

Psalm 5:12 says, "You bless the godly, O LORD, surrounding them with your shield of love" (NLT). As we take refuge behind that shield by walking in the strength of God's love, we're surrounded by a supernatural barrier that nothing can penetrate. We're fully protected and set free in every situation to act and react in love.

There's a story about a great theologian who was once asked, "Out of all the studies you've done and the commentaries you've written, what would you say is the greatest spiritual truth you've discovered?" The question was intended to be challenging. But the theologian answered it without a moment's hesitation.

Bursting into song, he said, "Jesus loves me, this I know, for the Bible tells me so."

Truly, that's the greatest revelation any of us can have. It always has been and always will be revolutionary. And it's unique to Christianity. No other religion or spiritual sect has ever presented a God that loves people with such intensity. The religions of the world offer gods that must be served out of fear; gods that must be appeased and have their needs met by human beings.

But our God has no need. He loves us because that's who He is and what He wants to do. It's His nature to love us—for ourselves and in spite of ourselves.

Our part is to simply receive His love by faith and give it to others. In this we find our greatest joy.

7

BY FAITH, NOT FEELINGS

Love is patient and kind. Love is not jealous or boastful or proud or rude. Love does not demand its own way. Love is not irritable, and it keeps no record of when it has been wronged. It is never glad about injustice but rejoices whenever the truth wins out. Love never gives up.

1 Corinthians 13:4-7, NLT

"Dennis, I know everything you've been saying about God's love is in the Bible," you might say. "But the problem for me is, sometimes I just don't feel very loved—or very loving, either, for that matter. So what am I supposed to do?"

Just walk by faith. Don't let yourself be fooled by feelings. God loves you all the time—when you feel like He does and when you don't. So you can love others all the time, too. And as you do, God will do amazing things for them through you.

I remember one time when I personally saw this proven in an especially dramatic way. I was ministering at a series of meetings at church in Australia with a number of other ministers. One of them was particularly well-known for his healing anointing, and I was speaking the night before his well-advertised healing service was scheduled to take place.

Although I'd prepared for my message as usual, when I walked into the service that evening, I didn't have the sense of excitement about it I sometimes have. I didn't feel especially "in the zone," you might say. I felt kind of blah.

I wasn't especially concerned about this. I've ministered for years, and I know how to step up by faith and do my job. So that's what I intended to do. Just before the service began, however, the Lord said something that threw me. He said, "Tonight I want you to pray for the sick."

What?

"Lord, the healing service is tomorrow night!" I argued. "They've been announcing it all week. Brother So-and-so will be laying hands on people, and everybody wants him to pray for them. If I call for people to receive healing tonight, nobody will come!"

The Lord, of course, wasn't concerned about any of this. He just kept telling me to pray for the sick. So that's what I did. With a bit of explanation and feeling insecure, I offered to pray for anyone in the congregation who needed healing. To my surprise, almost everybody responded. They lined up at the front of the church and down the aisles.

The first person in the prayer line who caught my eye was a woman who appeared to be in terrible pain. Wearing a brace on her back and braces on both legs and arms, she grimaced in pain with every move. She'd been sitting on the second row, and the people on the first row had pushed aside their chairs so she could get to the front with as few steps as possible. As a result, the attention of the whole congregation was focused on her.

I decided right away I'd start by praying for her. I wish I could tell you this was because I was confident she'd receive an instant miracle. But it wasn't. Although I hate to admit it, I wanted to pray for her first because I saw she was hurting and I wanted her to be able to get back to her chair and sit down.

Emotionally, I still wasn't feeling anything. But the Bible says, "Lay hands on the sick and they will recover" (Mark 16:18). So I laid hands on her by faith and prayed. Then I went on and ministered to the rest of the people. Some of them responded by falling under the power of God. Some lifted their hands and began to cry. Others shouted and thanked the Lord. A few did absolutely nothing. As for me, I continued to feel as dry as the Australian Outback the whole time.

After I'd finished praying for everybody, I turned the meeting back over to the pastor and sat down. He was wrapping up the service when suddenly he was interrupted by a commotion on the second row. Once again, people had started moving chairs aside to make way for the lady wearing the braces. Only this time, as she came forward, she was pulling those braces off and everybody was shouting.

It turned out the entire church knew this woman. She'd been suffering for eight years from a botched surgery, and they were all aware of what she'd been going through. So when they saw that she was healed, they started rejoicing. So did I! I hadn't felt a thing since the service began. But when that woman started running around without those braces, I jumped and hollered like everybody else. We all felt like we were in the zone then!

God, of course, had been in the zone the whole time. He's always in the zone. He's always loving people. So if we'll do what He says, He'll consistently pour His love through us and touch people's lives. We don't have to wait for some kind of special emotion or feeling; as children of the King we always have the right and capacity to obey His royal law of love. We can walk in that love 24/7 because it's on the inside of us. It's one of the grace laws that have been written in our heart!

LOVE LIBERATES

Of course, living by the law of love doesn't always mean doing something as dramatic as praying for a crippled person and seeing God heal them. Many times, it just involves being kind. It's the little things—like a caring smile, a small act of generosity, or a kind word—that lift people's spirits on a daily basis. It's loving them more than they deserve. Responding with gentleness and understanding when they're angry, hurt, or frustrated. Holding our peace when they lash out and give us a piece of their mind.

The Bible puts a high priority on such acts of kindness. It says of the virtuous woman in Proverbs 31, for instance, that "she opens her mouth with wisdom, and on her tongue is the law of kindness." Or as the *New Living Translation* says, "When she speaks, her words are wise, and kindness is the rule when she gives instructions."

The same thing could be said of a virtuous man. Any weakling can cave in to pressure or frustration and react by spewing mean, cutting words. But it takes a man of strength and character to respond with gentleness, and diffuse a potentially explosive situation. It takes a mature Christian to deal with difficult people while still obeying Scriptural instructions like these:

- Let your speech always be gracious, seasoned with salt, so that you may know how you ought to answer everyone(Colossians 4:6, RSV).

- ...With all lowliness and gentleness, with longsuffering, bearing with one another in love, endeavoring to keep the unity of the Spirit in the bond of peace (Ephesians 4:2-3).

- Put on tender mercies, kindness, humility, meekness, longsuffering; bearing with one another, and forgiving one another; if anyone has a complaint against another; even as Christ forgave you, so you also must do (Colossians 3:12-13).

Although it's not necessarily easy in all situations to treat people with this sort of kindness, by God's grace you can always do it. And when you do, you'll be amazed at how it liberates those around you. They'll start feeling free to open up to you. They'll know they can trust you; that you care about them and want to bless them.

They'll also be much more receptive to hearing what you have to share with them about the Lord. They won't be likely to think you're judging them or looking down on them, so you'll be able to talk to them about Him without being afraid they'll get mad or be offended.

A lot of Christians worry about that, and it hinders them from telling people about Jesus. *How can I witness to people without making them feel like I'm just ramming religion down their throat?* they wonder.

To me, the answer seems obvious. Don't ram religion down their throat! Instead, be kind to them. Express your interest in them. Smile at them, ask them about themselves, and really listen to what they say.

When you take that approach, you'll be shocked at how positively people respond. Instead of pushing you away, they'll be drawn to you. They'll be inclined to believe you when you tell them God loves them and wants them to know Him, because they've already sensed His love for them through you.

LOVE FORGIVES

Another way we cooperate with the royal law of love is through forgiveness. Whenever somebody does us wrong we make the choice to forgive them—and forgive them completely. We don't take the attitude the world does and say, "Well, I'm going to forgive you but I'm never going to forget what you did. I'm going to keep it in mind and make sure you never get a chance to do it again." We don't live by the old adage, "Cut me once, shame on you. Cut me twice, shame on me."

No, we operate in the God-kind of love by doing for others what He's done for us. How has He forgiven us?

- As far as the east is from the west, so far has He removed our transgressions from us (Psalm 103:12).

- Our sins and lawless deeds He remembers no more" (Hebrews 10:17).

- In Christ, God has reconciled us to Himself, no longer counting our sins against us (2 Corinthians 5:19, NLT).

Those verses don't mean that God is oblivious to our sins. He's not. He's fully aware of all the bad things we've done. He simply chooses not to bring them up and hold them against us. He chooses to deal with us as the righteous, even though He knows we've all been sinners, because that's what love does. The love of God forgives and treats people as if they'd never sinned.

We, as believers, are commanded to treat people the same way. The Bible leaves no doubt about it. It says, "If you have anything against anyone, forgive him, that your Father in heaven may also forgive you your trespasses...As the Lord forgave you, so you must forgive others" (Mark 11:25, Colossians 3:13, NLT).

To be clear, I'm not saying the Lord expects us to put up with abusive situations. If someone is habitually hurting us, we should take the necessary steps to protect ourselves. As the Lord leads, we may have to love certain people from a safe distance. But we don't seek revenge. We don't remind them and everybody else of their sins all the time.

We don't go to God and ask Him to punish those people, either. Instead, we forgive them when we pray. We ask the Lord to bless them and have mercy on them just as He has had mercy on us.

I know what you might be thinking. *That just doesn't seem fair! There are people in my life who've done things that really hurt me!*

I'm sure that's true. But if you don't forgive them, those things will hurt you even more because unforgiveness is toxic. Your system isn't created to handle it. As one leading neuroscientist says, "Human beings are literally hardwired for love." We're physically and neurologically designed to live by it. So when we violate the laws of love by holding grudges against people and hanging onto the fear that they'll hurt us again, it messes up our mental wiring. It creates chaos and havoc in our brains, and in a sense, it causes brain damage.

What's more, because the brain regulates the other systems of the body, if we keep clinging to fear and unforgiveness, other bad things start to happen. Our brain reacts to the negative stress we're putting on it and floods our system with harmful chemicals that suppress our immune system, upset our digestion, and cause all kinds of problems.

By embracing and walking in the God-kind of love, however, we can shut down this toxic cycle. We can live like He designed us to live. We can do for others what He did for us. We can forgive them, let go of the sins they committed against us, and step into a whole new realm of freedom.

LOVE GIVES

One final quality of the God-kind of love that I want to mention is this: It not only liberates and forgives, it also gives. Giving, more than anything else, is the hallmark of God's nature. He so loved the world that He gave; and the more we grow up in Him, the more we follow in His footsteps. We become less and less focused on getting and taking. We stop thinking so much about *Who's going to give to me?* And start asking instead, *What can I give to others that's of value? Can I give wisdom? Can I give words of encouragement? Can I give my finances?*

I realize some believers stress out when they hear this. They say, "Please don't talk to me about giving! Right now, I need to be on the receiving end of somebody else's giving. I need God to get some stuff to me, not show me how to give to everybody else."

I understand those sentiments. I've had them myself. There have been times when the Lord instructed me to give that I definitely felt like I needed to be getting instead. I remember one particular time early in our ministry when Vikki and I were really on the edge where money was concerned. We barely had enough to get by. During a conference we were attending, we found out one of the ministers there needed a really big financial miracle—$150,000 by the end of the following week—and the Lord told us to bless him with $1,000.

At the time, we didn't have that much to give. But here's what the Lord instructed us to do. He told me to go talk to the man and say, "I'm going to send you $1,000, and I'm going to send it in the next ten days."

The man responded to me in a way that was cordial and kind. He thanked me and was gracious, but I could tell what he was thinking. I didn't have the resources to solve his problem. He needed 149 other people to make the same commitment.

I didn't blame him for his less-than-enthusiastic response, and it really didn't bother me. The only reason I'd spoken to Him was because I wanted to obey the Lord. I wanted to let Him know I was committed to doing what He'd asked.

"Wasn't it hard for you to make that commitment?" somebody might ask.

Not really. Although Vikki and I both struggled a little with it initially, once we made the decision to give, the Lord energized us with His grace and made it the easiest thing we ever did. He not only provided us with enough to give the $1,000 within the designated time frame, He blessed us financially and took care of our needs as well.

In the years since, He's done the same kind of thing time and again. One time, He even asked us to give away our ministry airplane. I don't mind telling you, when He first dropped that thought into my heart, I wasn't very excited about it. I really liked that plane! I hadn't planned on giving it away.

But my attitude changed as I began thinking about the person who'd be on the receiving end of that gift. He was a minister who'd just come through a really tough time. The devil had gone after him and, through persecution, had stripped him of almost everything he had. I loved the idea of being able to give something to him that would be a part of his restoration, so I made up my mind to do it. The minute I did, the Lord backed my decision with the supply of His Spirit. I connected with His power and suddenly giving that plane away didn't even seem like a challenge. It didn't feel anymore like something I *had* to do. It became a thrill.

That's the way it always works for us, as believers. Because we have God's nature, giving comes as easy to us as breathing. All we have to do is tap into His grace by cooperating with His royal law of love.

8

SOLDIERS, FARMERS, AND ATHLETES

As each one has received a gift, minister it to one another, as good stewards of the manifold grace of God.

1 Peter 4:10

A grace-filled life is a blessed life. There's no question about it. The more you grow in your revelation of grace, the more you tap into it and cooperate with its laws, the more you're going to enjoy its benefits.

This doesn't mean, however, things will always go smoothly for you. It doesn't guarantee you'll just float effortlessly along and your life will be a picnic. On the contrary, as Jesus said to the first disciples:

In this world you will have trouble... (John 16:33, NIV).

I realize you already know this. Most every Christian does. Yet most of us would have to admit that the reality of it often catches us by surprise. When trouble actually shows up on our doorstep we tend to be shocked and upset. *Why is this happening?* we wonder. *I thought Jesus paid the price for me to have every good thing in life. I thought I was God's favorite child!*

If such thoughts have ever crossed your mind, let me assure you: No matter how rough the road of life may seem sometimes, you *are* God's favorite child. So am I. So are all His other born again sons and daughters. That's one of the awesome things about the Lord. He can look at each one of us and honestly say, "You're my favorite!"

As we've already established, however, that's not all there is to grace.

God's grace is not just His unmerited favor. It's also His divine influence upon our heart and the reflection of that influence showing up in our lives. It's the power He gives us to enable us to do what we would be unable to do on our own; a power that's been given to us for one very important reason: Because we need it.

We need it for God to be revealed in our lives and to bring forth His will on earth as it is in Heaven. We need it to fulfill our divine destiny. We need it because God has called us, as believers, to do things that, apart from His divine strength and ability, it would be impossible for us to do. We also need it because of this: Like it or not, some of the things we're called to do and go through will be extremely hard on our flesh.

Not exactly a thrilling thought, I'll admit. But it's true nonetheless. Second Timothy 2:1-6 confirms it. A key passage of Scripture when it comes to understanding the purpose of God's grace, it says:

> You therefore, my son, be strong in the grace that is in Christ Jesus...Endure hardship as a good soldier of Jesus Christ. No one engaged in warfare entangles himself with the affairs of this life, that he may please him who enlisted him as a soldier. And also if anyone competes in athletics, he is not crowned unless he competes according to the rules. The hard-working farmer must be first to partake of the crops. Consider what I say, and may the Lord give you understanding in all things.

Personally, I've found those are good verses to keep handy. They help prepare us for trouble so that when it inevitably arrives, instead of being surprised, we're ready to endure and overcome it with God's supernatural power. They also help remind us that such power isn't going to just fall on us like an apple off a tree. To lay hold of it and live by it, spiritually we'll have to apply the same kind of effort and diligence applied by people who dedicate themselves to the most vigorous natural vocations. We'll have to follow the examples set by:

- The soldier who endures hardship

- The competitive athlete

- The hard-working farmer

BORN FOR BATTLE

The first example, of a soldier in battle, is one that appears often in the New Testament. It's relevant to us, as believers, because we're engaged in a very real spiritual war. We're on this earth to advance God's kingdom, and that puts us in direct conflict with the forces of Satan.

This conflict is repeatedly referred to in the Bible in military terms. Time and again, it talks to us about things like waging the good warfare, fighting the good fight of faith, putting on the armor of God, and using our spiritual weapons to stand against the wiles of the devil.

Such terms resonate with us, as Christians. Even if we don't happen to be very military-minded, each one of us has the spirit of a spiritual warrior. We have within our born again hearts a desire to rise up like a mighty man or woman of God and do battle against the kingdom of darkness. It's part of our spiritual DNA. We're born to put the devil under our feet!

As thrilling as that sounds, however, it's serious business because the enemy we're facing is ruthless. He doesn't pull any punches or come after us with half-hearted attacks. He hits us with everything he's got. His goal is to completely overwhelm us and knock us out of the fight.

But he's also very crafty about it. Rather than coming after us consistently every day, he uses a more subtle strategy. He lets us rock along calmly for a season. He tries to trick us into dropping our guard and relaxing our grip on God's grace. Then one day when we're least expecting it and we think everything is going fine, he strikes out at our most vulnerable point. The next thing we know we're under a full-scale attack.

If you want to see what such an attack looks like, read Acts 27. It tells about an attack the devil launched against Paul when he was being taken as a prisoner on a ship to Rome to be tried in Caesar's court. You probably remember the story.

The first part of the journey went fine. The weather was nice. The water was calm and all was well. Then a bit of a contrary breeze kicked up. Although the owner of the ship wasn't concerned about it, Paul sensed a warning in his spirit. He prayed and the Lord showed him that if they kept sailing they'd run into trouble. Sharing this information with the people in charge of the ship:

> ...Paul advised them, saying, "Men, I perceive that this voyage will end with disaster and much loss, not only of the cargo and ship, but also our lives." Nevertheless the centurion was more persuaded by the helmsman and the owner of the ship than by the things spoken by Paul. And because the harbor was not suitable to winter in, the majority advised to set sail from there also, if by any means they could reach Phoenix, a harbor of Crete opening toward the southwest and northwest, and

winter there. When the south wind blew softly, supposing that they had obtained their desire, putting out to sea, they sailed close by Crete. (vv. 10-13)

Notice the Lord warned everybody in that situation about the danger that lay ahead. That's what He always does whenever a storm of some kind is coming. He alerts people in advance, when things are still peaceful and calm, so they can prepare and change course if necessary.

Many times, however, people don't spend enough time with God to hear His warning. Even if they do hear it, instead of pressing in to find out more, they often shrug it off. "I rebuke that thought," they say. "There's no storm ahead of me. Everything is going great right now. So I'm just going to keep going this way."

That's how the people on Paul's ship reacted. They felt the softness of the breezes and looked around at the palm trees swaying, and chose to ignore what Paul said. They assessed the situation in the natural, determined conditions were favorable, and decided to stay the course.

It proved to be a bad decision. Before long, "the weather changed abruptly, and a wind of typhoon strength...caught the ship and blew it out to sea" (NLT). Suddenly, there was no more soft wind blowing, no more palm trees swaying and gentle breezes ruffling their hair. Instead, the ship was being pummeled by hurricane-force wind. It was out in the middle of the water and the people onboard didn't even know which way they were going.

The storm raged on for many days, and eventually everybody lost all hope of surviving. Everybody except Paul, that is. He knew God had called him to go to Rome and testify before Caesar about Jesus, and that's what he intended to do. He wasn't about to fall short of his calling and drown in the middle of the sea just because the other people on his ship refused to listen to the Lord. So he just stayed in faith and stayed strong in the grace of God.

It's a good thing he did, too. Not only for his own sake but for the sake of all the other people on the boat. They wouldn't have had any idea of what to do if it hadn't been for Paul.

That just goes to show you: it's important to hang around the right people! They can help you through the storms of life. They can bring you into their safe haven if you happen to get hit by a circumstantial typhoon you're unprepared to handle. They can give you godly counsel, and if you'll apply it you can benefit from their spiritual strength, and in the end you'll be all right.

First Corinthians 15:33 says, "Bad company corrupts good morals." But the reverse can also be true. If you surround yourself with people who qualify as good company, they can show you how to make course corrections when you've gotten off track. They can help you get turned around when you're going the wrong direction.

That's what Paul did for the people on his ship. When they ran out of options and were ready to give up and die, he gave them hope and told them how to survive. He said:

Men, you should have listened to me, and not have sailed from Crete and incurred this disaster and loss. And now I urge you to take heart, for there will be no loss of life among you, but only of the ship. For there stood by me this night an angel of the God to whom I belong and whom I serve, saying, 'Do not be afraid, Paul; you must be brought before Caesar; and indeed God has granted you all those who sail with you.' Therefore take heart, men, for I believe God that it will be just as it was told me. (vv. 21-25)

TAKING CHARGE IN THE MIDST OF CHAOS

Those words were exactly what everybody needed to hear at that moment. They're the kind of words we all need to hear in the heat of a storm. When some devilish situation is threatening to overwhelm us, we need somebody with real faith to tell us to cheer up and have courage. We need somebody who has a living connection with God to remind us of His Word and say, "Listen up, now! God promised to keep us safe. He said He'd deliver us from this storm, and I believe it. If you'll believe it, too, and stick with me you're going to come through all right."

We can all follow the leading of the Lord much better when we have such spiritual coaching! And at times we all need it. But as believers, our goal is to mature to the point where we don't always have to be on the receiving end of it. We want to grow strong in grace so that, like Paul, we can take charge in the midst of chaos and give that kind of encouragement and direction to others.

Personally, I believe we're moving into a time now where increasing numbers of people will be looking to the Body of Christ for just such help. They'll be overwhelmed by the storms that are coming upon the world and won't know how to survive them. So they'll need us to use the authority God has given us and tell them what to do. That doesn't mean we'll just be ordering everybody around and blasting them with our opinions. It means we'll be sharing with them, in love, the wisdom of God so they'll know what to believe and how to act in order to make it safely through the storm.

Of course, even in stormy times, some people won't want to hear that kind of wisdom. They won't like what we have to say at all. Others will embrace it and apply it. But, either way, as God's people we're responsible to have His Word in our mouth and be willing to declare it as He directs. We're responsible before Him for what we choose to say and what we choose not to say.

In Acts 27, Paul made the right choice. He chose to speak the Word of the Lord; the people listened; and God spared them all.

Of course, the reason things turned out that way is because Paul had interceded for those people. He'd prayed for their deliverance, not only because he cared about them but because he knew the purpose of the storm. It had nothing to do with his hapless shipmates. It was a tool being used by the devil to stop Paul from reaching his God-ordained destination. The last thing Satan wanted was for Paul to get to Rome and spread the Gospel there to those in the highest places of governmental authority. So he'd attacked that ship and tried to kill everybody on it.

If you don't think that's the truth, you don't understand the kind of warfare we, as believers, are involved in. Satan will hold back nothing; he will do everything he can do to prevent you, as a believer, from fulfilling the destiny God has planned for you. He'll plot and strategize to strike out against you in the most savage ways.

He may not always be trying to literally kill you, but then he's not averse to that idea, either. Now that you've given your heart to Jesus, the devil isn't trying to keep you out of Heaven anymore. He wishes you'd hurry up and go. He wants you to get off this planet because you carry the authority and power of God, which is the only weapon that can effectively stop the spread of his demonic kingdom.

If the devil had his way about it, he'd kill you and every believer on earth right now. But he doesn't have the power. He can't take your life unless you give it to him. So he tries to mess you up in other ways. He tries to get you off in all kinds of strife and sin and unbelief. He uses whatever strategy he thinks will work against you. Wherever you're vulnerable to him that's where he's going to hit you. He's not looking for your strong points; he's looking for your weaknesses.

"But Dennis," you might say, "everybody has weaknesses!"

I know it. That's why we need to be strong in God's grace. It supplies us with supernatural strength in the areas of our lives where we're naturally weak. It puts within our grasp everything it takes to destroy and defeat every strategy Satan could ever devise against us.

This is what Paul was trying to get across to us in Second Corinthians 12. There, he wrote about a strategy the devil repeatedly used against him in an area of human weakness. Describing it as "a thorn in the flesh...a messenger of Satan to buffet me," he said:

> Concerning this thing I pleaded with the Lord three times that it might depart from me. And He said to me, "My grace is sufficient for you, for My strength is made perfect in weakness." Therefore most gladly I will rather boast in my infirmities, that the power of Christ may rest upon me. Therefore I take pleasure in infirmities, in reproaches, in needs, in persecutions, in distresses, for Christ's sake. For when I am weak, then I am strong. (vv. 7-10)

Sadly, a lot of good Christian people have misinterpreted those verses. They've somehow gotten the idea that God sent the thorn in order to keep Paul humble. They think that when he asked to be delivered from it, God refused and said, "No, Paul. You'll have to keep this demon a little longer."

But those people are mistaken. The attack was sent by Satan, not by God. And what God said when Paul asked him to make the devil stop attacking him was essentially this: *Paul, you have My grace, and that grace is enough to enable you to triumph over this strategy Satan is using against you. My strength is made perfect in your weakness. So the more you realize you are weak in yourself and look to My grace—My ability and power—the stronger you become.*

This is why we, as spiritual soldiers, need to be strong in God's grace!

If we're strong in grace, we don't have to stumble over the obstacles the devil throws in our path. We don't have to get tangled up in his deceptions or cave in under the pressures he tries to put on us. We don't have to give up and let Satan defeat us just because, in the natural, we're weak and limited. Instead, we can follow the instructions in Joel 3:10: "Let the weak say, 'I am strong.'"

Why should we say that? Not so we can just stay weak, but so that we can get our eyes off our weakness, off the threats of the devil, and onto

God's grace which imparts to us all the divine ability and strength we need to handle anything Hell can dish out.

This is real Christianity! It's continually accepting what you cannot do on your own and, at the same time, having full confidence in what Christ can do through you. It's saying, "Yeah, I'm finding out more every day about what I can't handle; but in Christ I can handle absolutely anything that comes along because He gives me more and more grace!" (James 4:6, AMP).

THE BUSINESS OF PRODUCING FRUIT

Now, keeping in mind how grace equips us to be effective spiritual soldiers, let's look at another example Second Timothy 2 tells us to follow: the example of the hard-working farmer.

I don't know if you've ever thought about it, but as believers, we have a lot in common with farmers. For one thing, farmers are in the business of producing fruit. They plant seed and raise crops, not only to feed themselves and their families, but to feed multitudes of people.

As believers, the same is true of us. We're in the business of producing fruit, too. We plant spiritual seeds and reap spiritual harvests—not just so that we can be blessed, but so we can be a big-time blessing in the lives of other people. We're called to use the divine abilities we've been given to minister to those around us, as First

Peter 4:10 says: "As faithful dispensers of the magnificently varied grace of God" (Phillips).

I like that phrase "magnificently varied." It highlights the fact that, just as different farmers have various kinds of natural seed to plant, each one of us, as believers, has been given different spiritual graces for service. For instance, I have a teaching gift. Another person might have a special gift for administration, or hospitality, or exhortation. Such gifts, to some degree, might come naturally to us. They might be talents and abilities we've possessed all our lives. But they become something divine and supernatural when we couple them with God's grace—which is what the Bible instructs us to do. It says:

> If anyone speaks, let him speak as the oracles of God. If anyone ministers, let him do it as with the ability which God supplies, that in all things God may be glorified through Jesus Christ, to whom belong the glory and the dominion forever and ever. (1 Peter 4:11)

God isn't glorified when we serve Him with just our own talents and ideas. He only gets glory when we serve Him with the ability He supplies. If we depend on our ability, we actually "frustrate the grace of God" (Galatians 2:21, KJV).

What exactly does it mean to frustrate His grace?

It means to have it and do nothing with it. In farming terms, it means to have seed and not bother to plant it, and therefore fail to produce fruit.

"Well, I'm busy working for God all the time," somebody might say, "and I still don't see much fruit-producing going on in my life!"

Then you're just operating in the flesh. You're just doing what you can do. God hasn't called you to do what you can do on your own; He's called you to do what, without Him, you cannot do. He's called you to do what can only be accomplished through His involvement and through complete commitment to and dependence upon Jesus. If you're spending all your time accomplishing things in your own strength, you're missing out on the whole deal. If you don't have a vision that exceeds your own abilities, it's very likely you've never discovered your true, God-ordained calling.

"But Dennis, I do have a big vision. I have it in my heart to do a great deal more for the Lord than I could ever get done on my own. But I'm still not making any progress. Is there something else I might be missing?"

Yes...and you might find out what it is by considering another example the New Testament encourages us to follow.

The example of the athlete.

GOD'S WAYS BRING GOD'S RESULTS

The two characteristics of the successful athlete specifically mentioned in Second Timothy 2 are these: First, the athlete competes; he presses toward the goal with the intention of winning the prize. Second, he does it according to the rules of the game.

Although I hate to have to say it, those characteristics are not necessarily common among believers. Many want the kind of victory that comes through relationship with Jesus, but they don't really want to do what it takes to obtain that victory. They want the blessings that come through obedience; they just don't want to obey God. They want the results of faith; but they don't want to live by faith. They want God to intervene in their situation; they just don't want Him to interfere with what they're doing.

That's not how things work. We're not going to experience success in life by ignoring the divine rules of the game. We're not going to finish our race on this earth in triumph by just doing what happens to be convenient and hoping for the best.

Yet that's how a lot of Christians live. Take how they raise their children, for instance. They say, "Well, I'm trying to be a good parent. I hope what I'm doing turns out to be right." But they don't bother to seek God about it. They don't press into His wisdom and grace where parenting is concerned. As a result, they don't realize until after their little darlings grow up that they're a mess; and by then it's too late to do anything about it because their children don't want to hear a word they say.

That's a sad situation. If, as a parent, you get yourself into it, God will have mercy on you and help you out in the midst of it as much as He can. But let me ask you something: Wouldn't it be better to find out what works ahead of time, while you can still have a godly impact on your children? Wouldn't it give God more glory if you started when they were young, raising them in a manner that will cause them to be blessed?

The Bible will tell you how to do that. It will show you how to "train up a child in the way he should go" so that "when he is old he will not depart from it" (Proverbs 22:6). But it's your responsibility, as a parent, to seek out that wisdom and receive God's grace to apply it.

I don't mean to pick on parents, of course. The same principle holds true for all of us in every area of life. We shouldn't wait until our time on earth is over to find out whether or not we've been handling things properly. We shouldn't wait until reward day when we're standing before Jesus to know if we ran our race according to the rules.

We can open our Bible now, before the race is over. We can be like the wise farmer and plant today what we want to harvest tomorrow. As Galatians 6:7-9 says:

> God is not mocked; for whatever a man sows, that he will also reap. For he who

sows to his flesh will of the flesh reap corruption, but he who sows to the Spirit will of the Spirit reap everlasting life. And let us not grow weary while doing good, for in due season we shall reap if we do not lose heart.

Amazingly enough, that passage of Scripture aggravates some Christians. They don't want to accept the fact that what they sow is what they're going to reap. They don't want to believe that doing things God's way always produces God's results. Some years ago, one man got so upset with me for talking about it that he came up after the service and got right in my face. He wagged his finger at me and told me he'd believed God and done everything God told him to do, and yet God had failed to keep His promise.

That claim didn't even make me flinch. As far as I was concerned, it had zero credibility. No amount of finger-wagging in the world is going to convince me that God is unfaithful, and I told the man so. "The reason God's promise didn't come to pass for you, sir," I said, "is because you didn't do what He said to do. If you do what God tells you to do, the way He tells you to do it, His promises come to pass. That's all there is to it."

He didn't like that answer. So we ended the conversation agreeing that we disagreed.

I know what you might be thinking. *Isn't that a little legalistic? By telling that man he had to do something to experience the fulfillment of a scriptural promise weren't you putting him back under law and setting aside the grace of God?*

No, I wasn't setting aside God's grace. I was doing just the opposite. I was encouraging the man to activate the power of that grace in his life by tapping into it to do what God told him to do.

To understand why that's not legalistic, think back about what we learned earlier from John 1:17. It says, "The law was given through Moses, but grace and truth came through Jesus Christ." As you'll remember, we established in a previous chapter that the law brought truth to people, but it didn't provide them with the power to live that truth. It just showed them how far away from God's standard they really were.

That's what putting someone under the law does. It reveals sin to them, but it doesn't deliver them from it. It leaves them in bondage, knowing what God said to do and yet unable to do it.

Because of Jesus, however, we aren't in that position anymore! He freed us from that kind of bondage because He not only brought truth, He brought grace. What is grace? It's the power to live the truth. It's the ability, not to keep a list of legalistic laws, but to live in the spirit of the Person who *is* the Truth, the Lord Jesus Christ.

Many Christians haven't really grasped this. They think Jesus came to earth to keep the law on our behalf so that we could be free from it. But what He actually did was "fulfill" the law (Matthew 5:17) and then provide for us an infinite supply of His grace so "that the righteous requirement of the law might be fulfilled in us," too (Romans 8:4).

Keeping the law and fulfilling the law are two very different things. Keeping the law is what people did under the Old Covenant. The Ten Commandments told them, "You shall not steal" (Exodus 20:15) so they tried not to steal. The Commandments told them, "You shall not murder" (v. 13), so they tried not to murder anybody.

But that's not what Jesus did. He didn't just keep the law, He fulfilled it. He didn't just "not steal" from people, He *gave* to everyone who would receive. He didn't just "not murder" people, He gave them *life*!

Now it's our turn. Jesus has imparted His righteousness to us and given us His limitless grace so that we can live like He did. "He who believes in Me," He said in John 14:12, "the works that I do he will do also; and greater works than these he will do, because I go to My Father."

How can we possibly live like Jesus lived and do His works?

We can't. Not in our own strength, anyway. But then, it's not our own strength He expects us to depend on. It's the wonderful power of His grace.

9

THE KEY OF DAVID

But now...the LORD has sought for Himself a man after His own heart, and the LORD has commanded him to be commander over His people.

1 Samuel 13:14

While God can do amazing things for you, and through you, as you grow in His grace, there is one thing I want to make clear: tapping into the power of grace will not turn you into a perfect human being who never makes another mistake. As delightful as that would be, it's not going to happen. No Christian on earth does everything perfectly. Nobody has all the answers and handles everything exactly right.

Not you. Not me. Not anybody.

As believers, we're still under construction in some area of our lives. We're all in the process of learning and growing up into the likeness of Jesus. None of us have matured to the point where we can say, "Yes, I've made it. I've reached spiritual perfection and now I'm absolutely Christ-like in every way." Although we may have made a lot of spiritual progress in our lives, the best any of us can say about ourselves is what the Apostle Paul said:

> Not that I have already attained, or am already perfected; but I press on, that I may lay hold of that for which Christ Jesus has also laid hold of me. (Philippians 3:12)

Personally, I'll be forever grateful to Paul for penning those words. It comforts me to know that even while he was impacting the entire known world with the Gospel, he himself still had some spiritual growing to do. Because I'm aware of my own shortcomings, that really encourages me.

I do wonder sometimes, though, if Paul were ministering today how people might react to him making such a public admission. If he said from a church pulpit some Sunday morning that he wasn't yet perfect, it might cause some problems. A lot of believers these days think they can only receive spiritual wisdom and edification from absolutely flawless people. So, if they find out that their pastor or some other spiritual leader they respect has some faults, they fall apart. They think they have to go somewhere else and find somebody who's exactly like Jesus so they can learn something from them.

God, however, doesn't act that way. He isn't going around looking for perfect people to represent Him to the world and show forth His glory. He's looking for imperfect people who will get a revelation of His grace and grow in it until it makes them great.

Not perfect.

But great.

Greatness is something every human being longs for. We were designed for it by God Himself. He has a great plan for every single person. He wants us all to connect to Him so He can reveal His greatness to us and show us how great we can become in Him.

Even unbelievers can sense this. That's why they're always chasing after significance and purpose in their lives. For some, the chase involves trying to climb the corporate ladder. Others chase influence, money, or education. Different people seek greatness in a variety of ways. But without Jesus they can never really find it.

Sadly, sometimes Christians don't, either. Even though they've given their hearts to the Lord, their longing for spiritual significance remains unsatisfied. They try their best to do good things, but they can't seem to find the spiritual keys that will take them from *good* to *great*.

That's a frustrating situation to be in—and we've all been there at one time or another. Myself included. But I discovered something in the Bible that made a big difference for me. I found it in Revelation 3:7. There, giving words of instruction and correction to a number of New Testament churches, Jesus said this:

> These things says He who is holy, He who is true, He who has the key of David, He who opens and no one shuts, and shuts and no one opens.

As I was reading that verse one day, the phrase *the key of David* jumped out at me. I'd seen it many times before, but I'd never really paid attention to it. *I wonder what that means?* I thought. Knowing it must be important, I did some studying and found out there's no specific definition of it in the Bible. There's lots of speculation about it by commentators and theologians but there's nothing in the Scriptures that says, "This is what the key of David actually is."

So to understand it, I looked back at what the Bible says about David himself. I went through the familiar Old Testament accounts of his life to find out what this key was that he discovered. *What set him apart?* I asked. *What enabled him to be a great king, despite the fact that he was an imperfect person and sometimes caused trouble?*

You do remember that David caused trouble, right?

Some very...serious...trouble.

IMPERFECT DOESN'T EVEN BEGIN TO DESCRIBE IT

Take, for instance, what happened between him and Bathsheba. In that situation, David not only committed adultery, but when he found out Bathsheba had gotten pregnant as a result of it, he arranged for her husband to be killed—even though the man was one of the most loyal officers in David's army!

To make things even worse, Bathsheba's grandfather, Ahithophel, was David's dear friend and counselor. He'd been faithful to David for many years, through thick and thin. They'd worshipped the Lord together. They'd worked together. They lived next door to each other. They were as close as two friends can be. David knew Bathsheba was Ahithophel's granddaughter. Yet he wreaked havoc in her life anyway and, in the process, he violated not only her but his covenant partner, Ahithophel.

Imperfect doesn't even begin to describe David's behavior in this instance. What he did was almost beyond comprehension. Ahithophel never got over it. His bitterness toward David festered for years. Eventually, when presented with the opportunity, he conspired to put an end to David's reign.

Guess who his co-conspirator was?

David's son Absalom.

Absalom was bitter toward David, too. Not because of Bathsheba but because of yet another appalling failure in David's life that occurred when his son Amnon raped his daughter Tamar. Although David got angry when he found out what Amnon had done, he did nothing about it. He ignored the wrong that Tamar had suffered and, instead of bringing her rapist to justice, he turned a blind eye. Absalom, who knew all about the situation, was furious about it. He saw David's lack of action as weakness and ultimately plotted not only to dethrone him but to kill him, so that he himself could become king. The plan failed, of course. But even so, a lot of people died as a result of it.

Just think about what a mess David's imperfections created! His failures, cowardice, bad judgment, and twisted thinking not only brought forth calamity and sorrow in his own life, they brought it into the lives of many others.

That's the way it always is. There are always consequences to the things we do and most of the time we don't bear those consequences alone. Others often end up bearing them, too. Sometimes for the rest of their life. We usually don't think about this, however, when we're in the throes of yielding to some temptation of the devil. Because our flesh is basically selfish, we're usually thinking, *It's all about me!*

At some point, though, after we do things we know are wrong, reality always hits. We see the pain we've caused not only for ourselves but for the people around us. Worst of all, we realize we've disobeyed and dishonored the Lord.

That's what happened to David. Ultimately, he had to face what he'd done. He had to go through the agony of watching Bathsheba weep when the child they'd conceived died. He had to hear the prophet Nathan say to him, "Why, then, have you despised the word of the LORD and done this horrible deed? For you have murdered Uriah and stolen his wife" (2 Samuel 12:9, NLT).

At that dark moment in his life, David knew he didn't deserve to be considered great. In fact, according to the law, he didn't even deserve to live. He deserved to die. Yet that's not what happened. David not only lived and continued to reign as king, he is still known today as one of the greatest spiritual leaders in the Bible—a man God Himself referred to as "a man after His own heart" (1 Samuel 13:14).

What was his secret? What was the key to his victory and his success?

He had an astonishing two-fold revelation of the grace of God.

Yes, you read that correctly. David had a revelation of God's grace. Even though he lived under the Old Covenant, he'd learned how to tap into what Jesus brought in the New Covenant— the unmerited favor and enabling power of God.

David first discovered this power in the early years of his life, as a young shepherd, spending long days alone out in the field. There, watching over his father's flocks and fellowshipping with the Lord, he learned that when he looked to God for help He would empower him to do things that were beyond his natural, human ability. This discovery turned David into the most daring shepherd in history.

One time, for example, a lion snatched one of his sheep and, instead of running for cover, David ran after the lion! He grabbed it by its beard, snatched the sheep out of its mouth, then struck the lion and killed it. On another occasion, he did pretty much the same thing to a giant named Goliath.

You probably remember hearing about him. He was the Philistine that stood out on a battlefield for several days taunting the entire Israeli army. A monster of a man, he was a seasoned and skilled warrior who had killed many people. He wanted Israel's King Saul, who was head and shoulders above any other Israelite, to come out on the battlefield and fight him. But Saul was afraid to accept the challenge.

David was still just a shepherd at the time. But when he showed up on the scene to deliver some food to his brothers who were in the army, he started talking like he could take Goliath down. Saul heard about it and sent for him, but when he actually saw David, however, his heart sunk. The kid was just a teenager!

"You don't stand a chance against Goliath," Saul told him.

"You're mistaken, sir," David replied. "It's actually Goliath who doesn't stand a chance against me!"

"Okay, then," said Saul. "I need you to kill him!"

"No problem," David answered...and off to the battlefield he went.

When he got there, Goliath could hardly believe Saul had sent such an unworthy opponent. He felt insulted and indignant. What he should have felt, however, was fear. He should have run for his life because he never even got a chance to defend himself. Before he knew what was happening, David sunk a rock between his eyes, knocked him flat, jumped on top of him, cut his head off with his own sword, and put the entire Philistine army to flight.

NOT JUST A GREAT LEADER, A GREAT SERVANT

It's amazing enough that David, as an Old Covenant believer, had such a giant-slaying revelation of God's empowering grace. But what's even more amazing is this: He also had a revelation of God's love, mercy, and undeserved favor. He understood that when people sin, the Lord wants to forgive them, not punish them; He wants to deliver them, not destroy them; He wants to welcome them into His presence, and not reject them. This realization opened the door for David to have a deeply personal relationship with God.

That was almost unheard of in those days! Most people under the Old Covenant only had a relationship with the law. They had a relationship with a religious system. Even the priests couldn't hear from God directly. They had to receive His direction through the stones they wore as breastplates over their priestly garments.

David, however, was different. He could hear from the Lord within his own heart and mind. So when it came to understanding the true nature of God, David got it like nobody else did.

That's why when he sinned and had that perverted relationship with Bathsheba, instead of trying to hide his sin from God, he confessed it and cried out to God for forgiveness. He reminded God that He was a God of loving kindness and tender mercy. He said:

> Have mercy on me, O God, because of your unfailing love. Because of your great compassion, blot out the stain of my sins. Wash me clean from my guilt. Purify me from my sin. For I recognize my shameful deeds—they haunt me day and night. Against you, and you alone, have I sinned; I have done what is evil in your sight. You will be proved right in what you say, and your judgment against me is just...Purify me from my sins, and I will be clean; wash me, and I will be whiter than snow. Oh, give me back my joy again; you have broken me—now let me rejoice. Don't keep looking at my sins. Remove the stain of my guilt. Create in me a clean heart, O God. Renew a right spirit within me...Forgive me for shedding blood, O God who saves; then I will joyfully sing of your forgiveness. Unseal my lips, O Lord, that I may praise you. You would not be pleased with sacrifices, or I would bring them. If I brought

you a burnt offering, you would not accept
it. The sacrifice you want is a broken spirit.
A broken and repentant heart, O God, you
will not despise. (Psalm 51:1-4, 7-17, NLT)

Notice in those last few verses David said that
God was more interested in what was going on
inside of a person than He was in outward sacrifices; that what God wanted most was for people
to be heartbroken over their sin so that He could
deliver them from it.

It's astonishing that David knew such things
about God in his day! Nobody else back then had
that kind of revelation. Yet David obtained it. He
chased after God until he found out what was in
His heart. Then he made God's heart his own by
not only receiving mercy and grace for himself
but by sharing it with others.

In other words, David followed God's example
and became not only a great leader but a great
servant.

Who exactly did David serve? you might
wonder.

First and foremost, he served the Lord. He put
God first and worshipped Him with whole-hearted
abandon. Read Second Samuel 6 sometime and
you'll see what I mean. It tells about the time the
Ark of the Covenant was brought back to Jerusalem after being captured by Israel's enemies.
The Ark carried God's presence. So as the priests
carried it into the city, David did something that
basically blew everybody's mind. He took off his

royal robes and "danced before the LORD with all his might" (2 Samuel 6:14).

David's horrified wife informed him later that he didn't look very kingly while he was leaping around and shouting praises to the Lord. But he didn't care what he looked like. He wasn't focused on trying to impress other people and make them treat him like a king. He was focused on serving God who had forgiven him, helped him, and returned the Ark of the Covenant to Israel.

David's commitment to serving didn't end with the worship service, either. He continued to serve God throughout his life by serving other people with the same startling abandon. Take for instance what he did for Mephibosheth. He was the crippled son of Jonathan, David's blood-covenant friend. He was also the grandson of King Saul who, for so many years, persecuted David and tried to kill him. After King Saul and Jonathan died, Mephibosheth was the only surviving member of the royal family.

According to the custom of the day, when David became king he should have considered Mephibosheth a threat to his throne and gotten rid of him. But he did just the opposite. He sent for him, not so that he could kill him, but so he could bless him.

Mephibosheth, uncertain of David's intentions, approached the situation with considerable trepidation. Shaking in his sandals...

When he came to David, he bowed low in great fear and said, "I am your servant." But David said, "Don't be afraid! I've asked you to come so that I can be kind to you because of my vow to your father, Jonathan. I will give you all the land that once belonged to your grandfather Saul, and you may live here with me at the palace!" Mephibosheth fell to the ground before the king. "Should the king show such kindness to a dead dog like me?" he exclaimed. (2 Samuel 9:6-8, NLT)

If you want to see the key of David in action, that's it right there. He took the mercy, power, and blessing God had poured out on him, and poured it out on someone else who didn't feel they deserved it. Rather than using his position as king to destroy Mephibosheth or to demand his service, he honored Mephibosheth and restored to him what he had lost.

JESUS' FORMULA FOR GREATNESS

Although that's an Old Testament story, it illustrates a New Covenant principle: people after God's own heart function best by serving, not by being served. Therefore, serving is the key to greatness in the Kingdom of God.

Jesus taught this time and again during His earthly ministry. Consider, for example, what He said about it to His disciples in the tenth chapter of Mark. There, James and John came to Him and said:

> Teacher, we want You to do for us whatever we ask. And He said to them, "What do you want Me to do for you?" They said to Him, Grant us that we may sit, one on Your right hand and the other on Your left, in Your glory. (vv. 35-37)

I have to admit, I used to judge James and John pretty harshly when I read those verses. I saw them as just being selfish, trying to undercut the other disciples and get a place of prominence in Jesus' kingdom. But really, what they wanted was the same thing David once wanted. They wanted to be great. That's what we all want. We want to feel like we're significant and important, that our life really does mean something. We want to be valued and recognized.

What's more, as believers, we want to be as close to the Lord as we can get; and James and John had the same desire. Growing up in Jewish society, they'd been taught, as all young people in Israel were taught, that when the Messiah rose to power He'd do wonderful things for the nation. He'd right wrongs and restore dignity to their society. So, believing they'd found the Messiah, James and John wanted to be a part of what He was about to do. They wanted to share in His greatness, not just for their own sake but for the sake of God's kingdom.

The problem was, however, that James and John left the other disciples out of the equation. And because the other disciples didn't appreciate this, a discussion erupted among them. (A discussion is what you call a fight when you're in church.) They all started debating about which of them were the greatest.

Of course, Jesus quickly settled the issue. But He didn't do it by rebuking them for desiring greatness. Instead, He told them how they could all achieve it. He said:

> You know that those who are considered rulers over the Gentiles lord it over them, and their great ones exercise authority over them. Yet it shall not be so among you; but whoever desires to become great among you shall be your servant. And whoever of you desires to be first shall be slave of all. For even the Son of Man did not come to be served, but to serve, and to give His life a ransom for many. (vv. 42-45)

I can only imagine how the disciples' faces must have fallen as they heard those words. The idea of being a servant probably wasn't very exciting to them. In their culture, people who were truly important didn't *become* servants, they *had* servants!

It's the same way today in countries all over the world. I remember a scene that confirmed this in Russia a few years ago. I was walking with another minister into a hotel restaurant and, as we were going in, a small crowd of people were coming out. The crowd was composed of one young lady surrounded by very big and intimidating-looking Russian bodyguards. As the entourage passed by, I noticed everybody stepped out of the way. They may or may not have known who the young lady was (I certainly didn't), but whatever her claim to fame, because she had these massive bodyguards around her acting as her servants, everybody treated her like she was "great." That's just how worldly society thinks.

As Christians, however, we're not supposed to think like worldly society. We're part of another society. We live in the kingdom of God, and in that kingdom, greatness isn't based on how many people we can get to serve us. It's based on how many people we can serve.

To think this way, however, we have to renew our minds. We have to stop seeing servanthood as something degrading, as a sign of inferiority and something to be embarrassed about. We have to get over the worldly idea that servants are failures and people who *have* servants are a success. In God's system, the opposite is true; and He wants us to learn how to live in His system the way He designed it.

He wants us to live in a way where, by serving, we become great.

Of course, He doesn't guarantee us that His kind of greatness will necessarily cause crowds to part for us like they did for the young lady I saw in Russia. He doesn't promise us the admiration of the world. But then, as disciples of the Lord, that's not what we're about. We don't do what we do so that other people will throw their accolades at us. We do it to please our heavenly Father. Regardless of what anybody else thinks of us, we want to be great in His eyes.

NO LAYMEN IN THE KINGDOM OF GOD

"But Dennis," you might say, "I don't see how I can really be of that much service in God's kingdom. I'm not called to full-time ministry like James and John and the rest of the 12 disciples were. I'm just an ordinary believer. I'm a just layman in the kingdom of God."

Actually, there's no such thing as *just a layman in the kingdom of God*.

According to Ephesians 4:12, all the "saints" (or believers) are to be equipped "for the work of ministry." So even if you're not an apostle, prophet, pastor, teacher, or evangelist, as a believer you're still a minister. And because, by definition, a minister is a server, that means you're called to serve God and to serve the Body of Christ in a significant way.

You're not supposed to just show up at the church picnic and serve people hot dogs or whatever. (Although that's a good thing to do.) You're supposed to serve, like the early disciples did, in a supernatural way. To minister to people by

God's grace. To pour out His mercy on them and bless them with His mighty power.

One way you do this is by operating in what 1 Corinthians 12:4 refers to as the "gifts" of the Holy Spirit. Translated from the Greek word *charisma*, which is derived from the Greek word for *grace*, the gifts of the Holy Spirit include the nine supernatural manifestations described by the Apostle Paul:

- The word of wisdom

- The word of knowledge

- The gift of faith

- The gifts of healings

- Prophecy

- Discerning of spirits

- Different kinds of tongues

- Interpretation of tongues

The Bible says such manifestations are "given to each one" of us, as believers. It says that, although none of us, as individuals, operate in all of them, the Holy Spirit distributes them among us, "individually as he wills" (1 Corinthians 12:11). As we believe that, make ourselves available to the Lord, and desire to be of service, He'll activate His grace gifts within us.

Most likely, if you've been walking with the Lord very long at all, you've already experienced this. You've already functioned in one or more of the gifts. They've probably worked through you even without your being aware of it. That's happened to me any number of times.

I remember one day in my office some years ago, for instance, I was just sitting there doing some work when I started thinking about a pastor I know named Paul. Realizing I hadn't talked to him in a long time, I thought, *I need to call him.* I picked up the phone and, as I started to dial his number, I suddenly remembered Paul had a radio broadcast. Seemingly out of the blue, the importance of it struck me. *That radio broadcast is blessing people,* I thought. *It's having a great impact on his town!*

When Paul answered the phone, we exchanged greetings and I shared what I'd been thinking. "I just want you to know your radio broadcast is having a good impact on your community," I said. Then I heard the phone hit the floor and had to wait while Paul danced around his office, shouting praises to God.

After a few seconds, he picked up the phone again. "Dennis?" he said.

"Yeah, man, I'm still here."

"Just before you called, I was praying about our radio program. I'd just told the Lord I didn't think it was having any impact at all. Then the phone rang and you told me it *is* having an impact!"

Isn't that interesting? I had no goose bumps or anything. I figured it was just my own idea to call up Paul and say something good to him. But really it was God's idea. It was the Holy Spirit giving me a word of knowledge. So what started out for me as just a phone call became something real supernatural for Paul. For him, it was the answer from God he was seeking. It was the voice of the Holy Spirit speaking to him.

That's how God wants to work through every believer. He wants it to be very natural for you to be spiritual, and very spiritual for you to be natural. He wants you to walk in His grace more and more so that serving other people supernaturally becomes the norm for you.

God never intended for the gifts of His Spirit to manifest through just a few special believers. They aren't primarily designed to operate in church buildings, through famous preachers who stand up on a platform or in front of television camera, while the congregation marvels them and says, "Oh, isn't he wonderful? Doesn't God do amazing things through him?" No, although I respect such ministers and have been blessed by many of them over the years, the members of the Body of Christ aren't supposed to be spectators watching God move through others. We're supposed to be participators who let God move through us as we're going about the business of our daily lives.

God's will is for all of His people to be ministers in His kingdom!

That's part of the revelation David received as a shepherd boy fellowshipping with God out in the fields. It's the reason that when he eventually built the tabernacle to house the Ark of the Covenant, he didn't model it after the Tabernacle in Exodus. He didn't set it up so that only a select group of people could go into it. Although he reverenced the plan for that Temple, he did something different. He opened up the tabernacle so that *everybody* could come into God's presence.

Think of it! David reached forward in time and built a place of worship that was based on the ministry of Jesus!

Why was he able to do it?

Because, even though according to our chronology Jesus hadn't yet come to earth, He is the "Lamb slain from the foundation of the world" (Revelation 13:8).

Somehow David caught hold of this. As a result, his Old Covenant tabernacle so reflected the spirit of the New Covenant that it's mentioned in the fifteenth chapter of Acts. There, when Jewish legalists in the early Church tried to exclude the Gentile believers from the Body of Christ, the Apostles reminded them of David's tabernacle. They quoted the words of the Old Testament prophet, through whom God said:

> I will...rebuild the tabernacle of David, which has fallen down; I will rebuild its ruins, and I will set it up; so that the rest

of mankind may seek the LORD. (Acts 15:16-17)

No wonder Jesus referred to the key of David in Revelation 3:7! No wonder He said, "These things says He who is holy, He who is true, He who has the key of David, He who opens and no one shuts, and shuts and no one opens." David understood that because of God's great heart of love, every believer can stand before God in the same authority, the same dominion, the same righteousness that Jesus Himself has.

Under the New Covenant, David's key has been put within the reach of all mankind. Because of the Lamb, the door to God's presence is open. Because of Jesus, we can all stand in God's grace...and serve...and become great.

10

PARTICIPATE WITH THE HOLY SPIRIT...AND GO GLOBAL

The grace of the Lord Jesus Christ, and the love of God, and the communion of the Holy Spirit be with you all. Amen.

2 Corinthians 13:14

If you've ever experienced the thrill of serving as a conduit of God's grace in someone else's life, you've already discovered it's downright addicting. Even when it happens seemingly by accident (like it did to me the day I called Pastor Paul about his radio broadcast), there's something marvelous about being used of the Lord to bless another person in a supernatural way. It reawakens you to the significance of your role in the plan of God. It reaffirms your divine call to bring Heaven to earth in the life of someone in need.

It also leaves you wanting more.

- More opportunities to show forth God's power and love.

- More people to bless

- More divine ability to minister to others the amazing goodness of God

Once you see somebody changed, encouraged, healed, or delivered because the power of God's grace touched them through you, you can't be satisfied sitting on the sidelines like a spiritual spectator watching what God is doing in the world. You want to spend more time in the game. You want get off the bench, so to speak, and live your whole life on God's supernatural playing field.

The question is: How do you go about that? Are you supposed to just spring into action and set things in motion yourself? Or should you wait for the Holy Spirit to lead the way?

Actually, you're supposed to do both. It's a joint operation. You increasingly become a channel of God's divine power by working together with Him through what Second Corinthians 13:14 refers to as "the communion of the Holy Spirit."

The word *communion*, translated from the Greek word *koinonia*, means fellowship or participation. It tells us that, as believers, our relationship with the Holy Spirit requires our involvement and cooperation. We can't just leave everything up to Him. Even though we're dependent upon His power, He won't just move us around like checkers on a board. He won't take over our life and just automatically make things happen. We have to participate in the action because we have a part to play and some things to do.

First and foremost, for example, we must do something about our stinking thinking. We must get busy replacing our old, worldly thoughts with God's Word so that we think more like He does.

> For My thoughts are not your thoughts, nor are your ways My ways, says the LORD. For as the heavens are higher than the earth, so are My ways higher than your ways, and My thoughts than your thoughts. For as the rain comes down, and the snow from heaven, and do not return there, but water the earth, and make it bring forth and bud, that it may give seed to the sower and bread to the eater, so shall My word be that goes forth from My mouth; it shall not return to Me void, but it shall accomplish what I please, and it shall prosper in the thing for which I sent it. (Isaiah 55:8-11)

Notice in those verses God just tells us straight out, "You don't think like I do. You're thinking is lower than mine!" But He doesn't say it to insult us. He's giving us a divine invitation. He's saying, "Come up here to My higher way of thinking. Put My Word in your mind and in your mouth, so that we can work together and accomplish My will."

Coming up to God's way of thinking changes everything! When we think like He does, we don't put limits on what the Holy Spirit can do through us. We don't look at the resources we have right now to see whether or not we can fulfill the assignments He gives us. We don't look at our limited natural capabilities and say, "I'll never make it. I don't have what it takes. I'm not qualified."

Instead, we look at things from God's perspective. We think, *I can do all things through Christ who strengthens me. My God supplies all my needs according to His riches in glory by Christ Jesus, and He always leads me in triumph* (Philippians 4:13, 19; 2 Corinthians 2:14).

Sadly, that's not how many believers think. Although they're born again and new creatures in Christ Jesus, they're still stuck in the world's way of thinking. They want their lives to change, but rather than going to the Word and getting thoughts from God that will set that change in motion, they either keep thinking their own thoughts...or they just don't think at all.

One Christian businessman I know claims that the latter is the most common problem. He told his wife one time, "If I ever need a brain transplant, make sure I get a brain that belonged to a Christian. That way I can be sure it hasn't been used!"

He was joking, of course. But he did have a point. As believers, we sometimes just plow ahead in life without giving things much thought and assume everything's going to turn out okay. Then, if it doesn't turn out okay, we blame it on God. We say, "I don't understand this, Jesus.

Why didn't You do more to help me? How could You let me get into this mess?"

In reality, of course, Jesus was never to blame for the messes we've gotten into. He tried to protect us from them. He tried to get us to read our Bible and said to us:

I beseech you therefore, brethren, by the mercies of God...Do not be conformed to this world, but be transformed by the renewing of your mind, that you may prove what is that good and acceptable and perfect will of God. (Romans 12:2)

Let God re-mold your minds from within, so that you may prove, in practice, that the plan God has for you is good. (Phillips)

FOLLOWING HIS LEADINGS, MOVED BY HIS FEELINGS

Renewing our minds with the Word dramatically improves our communion with the Holy Spirit. It not only takes the limits off our thinking and helps us look at things from God's perspective, it also helps us recognize and cooperate with the Holy Spirit's leadings. He always leads us in line with the Word, so the better we know the Word, the easier it is for us to follow Him and understand what He wants us to do.

What's more, since our thoughts are connected to our emotions, as we renew our minds with God's Word, we develop the capacity to feel what He feels and be moved by His emotions. I realize some people might consider this shocking, but feelings and emotions are not bad! They've gotten a bad reputation because they cause so much trouble when they're under the domination of the flesh or the devil. But they're actually part of God's perfect design. He created human emotions. He gave us feelings because He has feelings!

Granted, God's feelings operate on a higher level than ours. He doesn't get offended like we sometimes do and He's never touchy or resentful. But otherwise, His emotions are very much like yours and mine. He can be grieved, for instance (Ephesians 4:30). He can rejoice with gladness (Zephaniah 3:17). He can be righteously jealous and, as Jesus demonstrated when He drove the swindling merchants out of the Temple with a whip, He can be angry (James 4:5, John 2:15).

What God is most famous for, however, and what He uses to lead us most often, is compassion. Although compassion itself isn't really an emotion, it gives rise to emotion. It generates within us feelings of tenderness and affection. It moves us to reach out to people in mercy and kindness. That's what happened in Jesus' ministry. Again and again, we see Him being moved with compassion for the multitudes and teaching them, or healing their sick, or feeding them when they were hungry.

As believers, when we're stirred by God's compassion, we're moved to do the same kinds of things. We're moved to minister God's love to someone. To lift up a person who's fallen. To meet a need. To get involved in situations that are crying out for God's grace.

If you've been walking with the Lord very long, you've probably done such things many times—often without even being aware of it. You might have just walked past someone one day and felt your heart go out toward them in love. Sensing they were discouraged, you might have smiled at them and said something encouraging. You might have been driving along in your car one day and thought about somebody you hadn't seen in a while. Feeling a surge of love for them, you might have thought, *Oh, I hope things are going well for them. I hope their life is good and they're being blessed!*

What's going on when those kinds of things happen? You're feeling God's feelings. Your emotions are being stirred by His compassion.

Talk about something that will get you out on God's supernatural playing field! Divine compassion will move you to bless people and touch their lives with God's grace to a degree you never dreamed possible. It will help you work with the Holy Spirit in increasingly powerful ways in every area of your life.

TURNING YOUR PRAYER LIFE INTO AN ADVENTURE

Take the area of prayer, for instance. As you tune in to the Holy Spirit by thinking God's thoughts and feeling His feelings, the Holy Spirit can turn your prayer life into an adventure. He can take you beyond praying about your own needs and the items on your personal prayer list, and empower you to pray what's on the heart of God.

While having a prayer list is fine, praying what's on God's heart takes things to a higher level. It enables you to step up to a place where God not only attends to what you pray, He also shows you what to pray for. He reveals to you the requests He wants you to make so that He can respond to those requests and do for people what He longs to do.

"I don't understand!" somebody might say. "If God wants to do something for somebody, why wouldn't He just go ahead and do it? Why would He wait for us to ask Him?"

Because He's set us, as believers, in a very powerful place. He's given us authority on earth and called us to be co-laborers with Him in the work of His kingdom. He's set up His system so that we must ask before He acts. If you need confirmation of this, just look at what Jesus said about it in the New Testament.

- Whatever things you ask when you pray, believe that you receive them, and you will have them (Mark 11:24).

- Ask, and it will be given to you (Matthew 7:7).

- If you ask anything in My name, I will do it (John 14:14).

- Ask, and ye shall receive, that your joy may be full (John 16:24).

Obviously, Jesus really wants us to ask!

"Yeah, but Dennis, I have asked and asked and asked...and sometimes it seems like God doesn't answer."

I know what you mean. We all have that experience at one time or another. But when we do, I assure you, God isn't the problem. The problem is on our end. If we ask and don't receive, it's because, as James 4:3 says, "You ask amiss." It's because we're off track somewhere. We're asking in unbelief or with a wrong motive, or we're requesting something that's contrary to God's will.

This is why it's so vital for us to involve the Holy Spirit in our prayer life. He helps keep our prayers on track. In addition to moving us to pray with divine compassion, He keeps our prayers in perfect alignment with God's will by bringing His words to our remembrance and leading us not only to ponder those words and learn from them but to actually pray them.

You're probably familiar with how He does this. He'll flash a specific scripture across your mind as you're lifting someone before the Lord, and you'll suddenly see how it applies to them. As you're seeking God regarding a certain situation,

He'll remind you of a verse that reveals to you exactly how to pray about it.

Such Word-inspired prayers are super powerful because God's words are jam-packed full of His power. They "are spirit, and they are life" (John 6:63). They produce faith in our hearts and give us confidence that we're asking for exactly what God wants us to have (Romans 10:17).

When it comes to praying God's Word, you don't always have to wait for the Holy Spirit to make the first move, either. Any time you like, you can choose a verse in the Bible that speaks to your heart and turn it into a prayer.

Take Isaiah 58:11, for example:

> The LORD will guide you continually, and satisfy your soul in drought, And strengthen your bones; You shall be like a watered garden, And like a spring of water, whose waters do not fail.

If you're praying for someone who has been struggling in their walk with the Lord, you can make that verse a prayer by saying, "Father, I'm asking You according to Your Word to guide their steps today so that they make the right decisions and go the right direction. Flood the dry places in their life with the rain of Your Spirit so that in every area their heart is well-watered and their soul is satisfied. Lord, You've promised in Your Word to do these things, and I know they're Your will for this person's life. So I ask You to minister these blessings to them. I thank You for it and give You all the praise and glory, in Jesus' Name. Amen."

That's a good prayer, isn't it? A prayer like that can turn Bible reading time into a Holy Ghost time—and it all came out of just one verse!

"But I don't have enough time to pray that way," somebody might argue. "My Bible reading program requires me to read several chapters a day. If I spent that long praying one verse I might not get all my reading done."

You might not. But wouldn't it be better to have one verse of the Bible come alive in you than to read several chapters and finish them without hearing from God? I certainly think so! Although I'm not against daily Bible reading programs, I've found that the Word that comes alive in me is the Word that makes the difference. And when I choose specific scriptures and take the time to speak and declare them in prayer, those scriptures come alive in me.

The reason for this is simple: As I pray the Word, I start actively participating with the Holy Spirit. I stir up my communion with Him. Then He starts moving and things get exciting.

I'm convinced that a lot of believers are bored with their prayer times because they don't do this. They don't partner with the Holy Spirit. They just plod along on their own. They pull a promise out of the Promise Box, or do whatever else they think they have to do to fulfill their religious duty. But they don't hook up with the Holy

Spirit and give Him the opportunity to refresh them and reveal Himself to them. So they never get over into what I call *The Power Zone!*

SPEAK GOD'S WORD AND RELEASE HIS POWER

What exactly is The Power Zone?

It's the spiritual zone you get into where, instead of asking God for something, you actually release His power with your words. It's the zone where, at the leading of the Holy Spirit, you deliver the Word of God as an authoritative command according to Mark 11:23, which says:

> Whoever says to this mountain, "Be removed and be cast into the sea," and does not doubt in his heart, but believes that those things he says will be done, he will have whatever he says.

God's Word, when released from your mouth, has creative power in it. It actually has the ability to go where you send it and create what you declared. I've seen this truth borne out time and again. Ministering in church services, for instance, I've received words from the Lord for people with specific diseases. He showed me what was wrong with them and then instructed me to say, "Be made whole, in Jesus' Name!" Through that simple declaration, God's generative power was released into people's bodies, and they were instantly healed.

As you participate with the Holy Spirit in prayer, your words can have the same kind of impact. They can be used to release God's power everywhere you go all day long. You can start out in the morning saying, "Lord, I ask You to help me be sensitive to Your Spirit today. I declare that, as one of Your sheep, I hear Your voice and follow your guidance in everything I do, say, and pray. Use me to be a blessing." Then all throughout the day, you can watch for and respond to the promptings of the Holy Spirit.

If He brings someone to your mind while you're sitting in your car, waiting to pick up your child from school, you can pray for that person however you're led to pray. If He puts some situation on your heart while you're in the break room at work, you can lift it before the Lord and say about it whatever the Holy Spirit gives you to say.

Spirit-led prayers don't have to be long to be powerful. The Apostle Paul sometimes prayed for people by just making "mention" of them to the Lord (Romans 1:9). So when the Holy Spirit puts somebody on your heart, if you don't know what to pray, just do what Paul did. Make mention of them. Say something like, "Father, I lift this person to You today. I just declare the blessing over them and their family. I declare Your hand is not only upon them but moving through them." If nothing else comes to you to pray, then you can assume nothing more is necessary.

As you watch for the leading of the Holy Spirit, however, sometimes He'll give you additional instructions. He might lead you to pray over an attack of Satan that has come against them, for instance. Even though in the natural, you might not know anything about it, you might find yourself interceding for them and releasing the power of God on their behalf by declaring, "I break the power of that attack in Jesus' Name!"

That kind of participation with the Holy Spirit can turn your whole life into a ministry. Everywhere you go, you can be a tool in God's hand—praying His prayers, feeling His feelings, and releasing the creative power of His Word. Without ever setting foot outside your city or your neighborhood or even your own home, through prayer you can go global for Jesus! You can minister God's grace to people in need, not just locally but all over the world!

I'm thinking right now of a time my wife, Vikki, was praying at home in our bedroom and she suddenly sensed a strong leading to pray for the son of a friend of ours, who was serving as a soldier in Afghanistan. As she yielded to that leading, the Holy Spirit moved on her with great intensity. She felt the young man was in danger and declared God's protection over him. It didn't take long. Just a few minutes and she felt a release.

Weeks later, we found out that on the day she prayed for him, our friend's son and his entire combat team came under severe attack. They were ambushed as they were going down the road. He turned out to be the only survivor.

I remember another time when Vikki was praying at home and two words kept coming up in her spirit. *Drug lords.* At first she didn't know what the Holy Spirit was trying to get across to her so she just kept repeating the words. "Drug lords...drug lords..." As she did, another phrase came up inside her. *Jesus is the Lord of Lords.* Instantly she knew what to pray. "Drug lords must bow to the Lord of Lords! Drug lords must bow to Jesus!"

That's all she said. Just two short sentences. In the natural, they didn't seem like any big deal. But spiritually, they were a very big deal. They were important because they'd come from God and been spoken in faith at the leading of the Holy Spirit.

Within the week, the news reports came out. One of the big drug cartels in Columbia had basically surrendered. They'd sent a letter to the Columbian government that essentially said, "We will dismantle our drug smuggling operation into America if you will guarantee we will not be extradited to the United States to stand trial."

It was an absolute miracle.

Up to that time, the only negotiating the drug cartels had done was with bombs. They'd "negotiated" by blowing up people, judges, and policemen. But God wanted to change that mess. He wanted to stop the flow of drugs from

Columbia into America—and He didn't want Columbia blown up in the process. So He came up with a better way. He found some people like Vikki (I'm sure she wasn't the only one but she was the only one I knew) who would pray. He found somebody who would obey the leading of the Holy Spirit and actually declare the Word of the Lord over the situation.

"But Dennis, what if I pray something like that and I don't ever find out what happened as a result?"

It doesn't matter. Just keep trusting God and keep obeying the promptings of the Spirit anyway. Just be happy to pray and do your part.

It's amazing what God can do through people who have that kind of attitude. He can use their prayers to affect countless lives. I heard a story about a particular minister who was ministering overseas. He was trekking across Tibet when a bunch of bandits attacked him. They assaulted him, stole all his goods, and intended to kill him, but he didn't die. Instead, after they left, he got up, got back on his donkey, and went back to preaching.

In the years that followed, he ended up traveling all over the world, winning multiplied thousands of people to the Lord. One day, he was telling a believer he'd met about some of his adventures. When he started telling the Tibet story, the believer got excited and grabbed his prayer journal. They compared notes, and the minister realized this believer had been praying for him at the exact time the bandits attacked him.

Think of it! The Lord used that person's prayer to save a minister's life and, as a result, multitudes heard the Gospel and were born again. Yet the person who prayed never would have known it this side of Heaven if it hadn't been for that seemingly chance meeting.

Remember that story next time the devil tries to convince you that you're not very significant in the plan of God. Remember it when you're hearing all the reports about what the big ministries are doing all over the world and you're tempted to think, *What difference does it make what I do?*

It makes a great deal of difference what you do!

You're part of the Body of Jesus Christ on earth. You're not only a recipient of His all-powerful grace, you're a carrier of it. So get out there on the playing field of life and set that grace in motion. Participate with the Holy Spirit in prayer.

Go global!

11

SURROUNDED AND PROTECTED IN THE PLACE OF GOD'S GRACE

Every God-begotten person conquers the world's ways. The conquering power that brings the world to its knees is our faith... The God-begotten are also the God-protected. The Evil One can't lay a hand on them.

1 John 5:4, 18, The Message

News reports about attempted robberies aren't generally very inspirational. But I saw one a few years ago I wish every believer in the world could see. The report concerned an incident that took place in the Dallas area, not far from where I live. Broadcast on local television station, it began with a video recorded by a surveillance camera in a small retail shop.

The first few seconds of the video showed grainy, black and white images of two women standing in the shop chatting. One of them, apparently a customer, was being waited on by the other, who was apparently the shop owner. Everything seemed to be quiet and normal. Just an ordinary day.

Then the door to the shop opened.

A man wearing a hood and brandishing a .45 pistol barged in. Pointing the pistol in the shop owner's face, he said, "Give me your money!"

The shop owner, pointing her finger right back at him, replied, "In the Name of Jesus, you get out of my shop."

It was clearly not the reaction the gunman expected. For a moment, he stood as if paralyzed and an unspoken question seemed to hang in the air: *Which is going to dominate this situation—the gun or the index-finger-backed-by-the-Name-of-Jesus?*

The robber glanced at the customer. "Oh, my God!" she cried. Then he looked back at the shop owner. Her finger was still pointed squarely in his direction. "Get out of my shop, in the Name of Jesus!" she repeated.

The video caught what happened next as clear as can be. The man bolted for the door and in a split-second, he was gone.

On the news broadcast, a reporter followed up the video with an interview with the shop owner (who was obviously a strong Christian) and the customer (whose faith wasn't quite as obvious, at least on that particular day). Both confirmed everything that happened. By the time they finished the interview, I was praising the Lord.

I've been telling about the incident ever since because it's a graphic picture of the supernatural protection God has provided for us, as believers. It shows the kind of deliverance from danger He's made available to us through the power of His grace. Such deliverance is vital in these last days. As Second Timothy 3:1 says, these are "perilous times."

The world is getting darker, and the devil is fighting us with everything he's got. As believers, we need to know God has us covered. We need to be certain that, as the God-begotten, we're also the God-protected. That we can go anywhere He tells us to go and do anything He tells us to do without any fear or trepidation.

In other words, we need to be sure we're living, surrounded and protected, 24/7, in the place of God's grace!

When we're living in that place, God can do absolutely amazing things for us. He can take care of us regardless of what's happening around us. Read Psalm 91 and you'll see what I mean. It says:

> He who dwells in the secret place of the Most High Shall abide under the shadow of the Almighty. I will say of the LORD, "He is my refuge and my fortress; My God, in Him I will trust." Surely He shall **deliver** you from the snare of the fowler and from the perilous pestilence. He shall cover you with His feathers, And under His wings you shall take refuge; His truth shall be your shield and buckler. You shall not be afraid of the terror by night, Nor of the arrow that flies by day, nor of

the pestilence that walks in darkness, Nor of the destruction that lays waste at noonday. A thousand may fall at your side, And ten thousand at your right hand; But it shall not come near you. Only with your eyes shall you look, And see the reward of the wicked. Because you have made the LORD, who is my refuge, Even the Most High, your dwelling place, no evil shall befall you, Nor shall any plague come near your dwelling; For He shall give His angels charge over you, To keep you in all your ways. In their hands they shall bear you up, Lest you dash your foot against a stone. You shall tread upon the lion and the cobra, The young lion and the serpent you shall trample underfoot. Because he has set his love upon Me, therefore I will **deliver** him [says the Lord]; I will set him on high, because he has known My name. He shall call upon Me, and I will answer him; I will be with him in trouble; I will **deliver** him and honor him. With long life I will satisfy him, and show him My salvation. (vv. 1-16)

Notice in those verses, God not only lists every possible kind of danger that might confront us, He promises three different times that He will *deliver* us from those dangers. Why does He make that promise three times? Because each time, in the original Hebrew text a different word is used.

In verse 3, which says God will "deliver you from the snare of the fowler," the Hebrew word that's used speaks of the kind of deliverance we experience when we get *ourselves* into trouble. It tells us that even if we fall into the devil's trap as a result of our own actions, the Lord will mercifully snatch us out of it. (Since most of us are pretty skilled at getting ourselves in trouble, we need that kind of deliverance a lot!)

In verse 14, which says "I will deliver him; I will set him on high, because he has known My name," the Hebrew word that's used refers to those times when the Lord lifts us up and carries us over trouble. It speaks of the kind of deliverance that enables us to avoid the devil's snares altogether. (Personally, I'm a big fan of this type of deliverance! When it comes to the schemes of the devil, I'm definitely into avoidance.)

In verse 15, which says "I will be with him in trouble; I will deliver him and honor him," the Hebrew word that's used refers to the deliverance we experience when, instead of being snatched out of trouble or avoiding it, we confront it. It speaks of those instances when we use the spiritual weapons God has given us and the authority of Jesus' Name and overcome the enemy's attacks.

WHEN YOU'RE OUT...YOU'RE IN

One person in the Bible who experienced all three kinds of deliverance on a regular basis was King David. As we've already seen, God was constantly delivering him from one danger or another. Whether David was battling a sheep-stealing lion, fighting the blood-thirsty Goliath, running from the murderous King Saul, fighting the forces of the Philistines, or facing a military coup engineered by his own son and his best friend...he always came out on top because he continually lived in the secret place of the Most High.

How did he manage to stay in that place? Given all the mistakes he made in his life and the dark, sinful moments he experienced, how was he able to abide continually under God's protective covering?

Psalm 32 explains it. There, David wrote:

Blessed is he whose transgression is forgiven, whose sin is covered. Blessed is the man to whom the LORD does not impute iniquity, and in whose spirit there is no deceit...I acknowledged my sin to You, and my iniquity I have not hidden. I said, "I will confess my transgressions to the LORD," and You forgave the iniquity of my sin. Selah. For this cause everyone who is godly shall pray to You in a time when You may be found; Surely in a flood of great waters they shall not come near him. You are my hiding place; You shall preserve me from trouble; You shall surround me with songs of deliverance... Many sorrows shall be to the wicked; but he who trusts in the LORD, mercy shall surround him. Be glad in the LORD and rejoice, you righteous; and shout for joy, all you upright in heart! (vv. 1-2, 5-7, 10-11)

Those verses make it clear, David accessed God's secret place of protection by using the same key we talked about earlier—*the key of David,* the key of divine grace!

Even though he lived in Old Testament times, David tapped into the New Testament revelation that God wasn't looking to punish people for their sin but to restore them. That God was in love with people and didn't want to hold their sin against them. That, because of what Jesus would do through the plan of redemption, if people would turn to God in faith, He would release them from their sin, deliver them from trouble, and cover them with His hand of blessing.

For all of us who want to dwell in the secret place of God's protection, this is a strategic revelation: God isn't holding things against us! Although, like David, we've all done some things wrong and had some dark, sinful moments, God still sees us as qualified for His protection because He Himself has made us righteous. He's delivered us out of the place of sin and put us in the place of His grace.

And in the place of grace, it's not about what we've done; it's all about what Jesus has done!

I saw this some years ago in a way I'll never forget. I was studying the book of Romans and noticed the word *sin* is used there not only as a verb to refer to an action, or as a noun to refer to a thing, it's also used to refer to a place. This surprised me. I'd never really thought of sin as being a place before. But the more I dug into the Scriptures, the more I realized there really is a spiritual place called *sin*.

It's a place we're all quite familiar with. Every one of us used to live there. Before we knew Jesus, we were trapped in sin like inmates in a prison, and no matter how hard we tried, we couldn't escape. Then we heard the Gospel. We received Jesus as our Lord and Savior, and He did for us what we couldn't do for ourselves. He unlocked the prison door, set us free, and we stepped out of the place of sin and into Him.

Talk about a major move! When you got born again, you moved into a whole new kingdom. You didn't just get your sins forgiven and a ticket to Heaven, you changed spiritual locations. That's a huge deal because unlike in the natural realm where there are all kinds of different places to be, in the realm of the spirit, there are only two options. You are either in the kingdom of darkness or in the kingdom of light. So once you move out of one, you are immediately in the other.

Do you realize what that means? It means once you move into Christ, you're out of the sin place and in the place of righteousness. There's no in-between place. No gray area. Once you're out, you're in!

Say it out loud right now. "I'm out of sin, and I'm in Christ. I'm in the place of right standing with God, and there's nothing the devil can do about it. Jesus has set me free from the cage of sin...and because I'm out, I'm in!"

"Yeah, but Dennis, I don't always act like I'm in Christ. Sometimes I do some things that aren't exactly Christ-like. Does that put me back in the place of sin?"

No, it doesn't.

The verb of sin, or the action of sin, can never rob you of your righteous place in Christ because you didn't earn your way into that place by your own good behavior; you were placed there by grace when you put your faith in Jesus. It's His righteousness you're standing in, and no mistake you make or sin you commit can affect it. Because you're in Christ, your spiritual location is secure. You're in the place of supernatural blessing and protection, the place where, as Psalm 32:10 says, "the Lord's mercy surrounds you."

THE GOD-BEGOTTEN ARE THE GOD-PROTECTED

Exactly what does it look like when God's mercy surrounds you?

You can see pictures of it all through the Bible, but one of my favorites is in Second Kings 6. It tells about a time God's mercy supernaturally surrounded the prophet Elisha. You probably remember the story. Elisha had gotten in trouble with the king of Syria who'd been trying to mount an attack against Israel. Every time he'd put together a plan and tell his troops about it, the Lord would alert Elisha, and he'd pass the information along to the Israelites. As a result, the attack would be thwarted.

When the Syrian king realized what was happening, he decided to put an end to Elisha's meddling by wiping him off the face of the earth. After finding out where Elisha was staying, "...he sent horses and chariots and a great army there, and they came by night and surrounded the city" (v. 15).

The next morning Elisha's servant woke up, went outside, and got the shock of his life! Rubbing the sleep from his eyes, he looked around and saw thousands of Syrian soldiers, armed and ready to strike. Imagine how he must have felt at that moment. Nervous wouldn't even begin to describe it. *This is the end!* he must have thought. *Prophet or not, Elisha's going down, and it looks like I'm going down along with him.*

Petrified, he cried out to Elisha, "Alas, my master! What shall we do?" (v. 14)

Oddly, Elisha answered without a trace of alarm. "Do not fear," he said, "for those who are with us are more than those who are with them." Then he prayed, and said, "LORD, open his eyes that he may see" (vv. 16-17).

Once the servant's eyes were opened, he saw the situation in an entirely new light. He looked into the realm of the spirit, "and behold, the mountain was full of horses and chariots of fire all around" (v. 17). Suddenly, it became obvious—Elisha and his servant weren't in trouble at all.

The Syrians were the ones in trouble. They were surrounded by the warring angels of Heaven and God's chariots of fire! Confronted with that kind of supernatural fire-power, the Syrians had no hope of capturing Elisha. They tried, but when they closed in on him, he simply said to the LORD, "Strike this people, I pray, with blindness" (v. 18).

The Lord did what Elisha asked, and as the Syrians stumbled around unable to see, Elisha tricked them. He said, "This is not the way, nor is this the city. Follow me, and I will bring you to the man whom you seek" (v. 19). Then with the Syrian army following him like a flock of sheep, Elisha led them to Samaria where the king of Israel took them captive.

When you're living in the place of God's grace, God will provide the same kind of supernatural protection for you! He'll send His heavenly hosts to deliver you from any threat that Satan can devise. He'll surround you with His power to such a degree that when the devil launches a strategy against you, it ends up working in your favor.

Of course, to get the full benefits of such protection, you have to cooperate with God. You can't turn your back and walk away from Him and expect it to work very well. But as long as you're trusting Him, obeying His instructions the best you know how, and repenting whenever you miss it, you can have confidence that He'll keep you covered at all times.

He's done it for me for many years now. Almost every week I travel to different places around the world, and sometimes I run into very dangerous conditions. Take, for instance, what happened one time when Vikki and I went to Russia to minister. We were scheduled to go first to St. Petersburg and then to Moscow, and while we were in St. Petersburg, the Chechnians started launching terror attacks. They blew up two airplanes at the Moscow airport and tried to blow up one of the city's subway stations. In the city of Beslan, in central Russia, an entire school was taken hostage and ultimately blown up.

By the time Vikki and I got to Moscow, the entire nation was in lockdown. People were being injured and killed. Much of the population felt threatened and insecure. The Russian President didn't know what to say, so for four days, he didn't address the situation publically at all.

Although I could sympathize with him, I didn't have that luxury. I had to minister that Sunday to a congregation at a church in Moscow, and the believers there needed answers. They needed encouragement and help, and I knew exactly what to say. I had an announcement for them. I told them God had them surrounded! I reminded them that the Bible says they're not only the God-begotten, they're the God-protected;

and He's promised to preserve them. I delivered to them the message of Psalm 121:

> I will lift up my eyes to the hills; From whence comes my help? My help comes from the LORD, Who made heaven and earth. He will not allow your foot to be moved; He who **keeps** you will not slumber. Behold, He who **keeps** Israel shall neither slumber nor sleep. The LORD is your keeper; The LORD is your shade at your right hand. The sun shall not strike you by day, nor the moon by night. The LORD shall **preserve** you from all evil; He shall **preserve** your soul. The LORD shall **preserve** your going out and your coming in from this time forth, and even forevermore.

GOD'S NOT SCARED

The Hebrew word translated *keep* or *preserve* in that Psalm means to hedge roundabout and to guard. I like that, don't you? I'm thrilled to know God has a hedge around me, and He's standing guard over me. I'm glad He promised me that He will preserve me from all evil.

All evil includes danger of every kind. It includes Satanic financial attacks and sickness and disease. As John 10:10 says, the devil comes "to steal, and to kill, and to destroy," and Jesus came so that we "may have life, and…have it more abundantly." So evil includes anything that steals, kills, destroys, or robs us of a long, abundant, satisfying life.

"Well, we do have to be realistic," somebody might say. "We can't really expect God to deliver us every time the devil attacks us."

Why not?

God said He'd deliver us from all evil, and we ought to believe it. We ought to expect Him to keep His promise to protect us, not only for our own sake but because that's what He wants to do. God doesn't just want to deliver us from Hell in the hereafter, He wants us to be delivered from every threat Hell brings against us right here on earth.

Protection is part of the blessing of salvation! We shouldn't let Satan rob us of it by filling us with fear. We ought to take advantage of what God has provided for us. No matter how much the odds might seem to be stacked against us in the natural, we should trust Him to keep us safe in any situation because He is well able to do it.

You may remember seeing the reports a few years ago on the national news about an Iranian pastor named Yousef Nadarkhani. He was arrested and imprisoned in 2010 for being a Christian and preaching the Gospel in Iran. Once in prison, he was given a choice: either renounce his faith in Jesus or be executed. He refused to renounce Jesus, so he was condemned to die.

Since, in the past, the ungodly government of Iran had not been shy about carrying out executions, the situation looked hopeless. But Christians began to pray about it nevertheless. They began to lay hold on God's delivering power for Pastor Yousef. Although he stayed locked up in prison for several years and the government kept threatening to execute him, believers kept praying.

In 2013, he was set free!

From a natural perspective, such an outcome should have been impossible. But God got it done! He's not intimidated by evil governments or prison bars or threats of execution. He's been protecting and delivering His people from those things for thousands of years.

Think again about what He did for King David in the Old Testament. David went to sleep some nights with entire armies trying to hunt him down and kill him. He lived through some tremendously tumultuous times. But God preserved him through it all because he kept declaring His delivering power. He kept saying, as he did in Psalm 3:

> LORD, how they have increased who trouble me! Many are they who rise up against me. Many are they who say of me, "There is no help for him in God." ... But You, O LORD, are a shield for me, My glory and the One who lifts up my head. I cried to the LORD with my voice, And He

heard me from His holy hill...I lay down and slept; I awoke, for the LORD sustained me. I will not be afraid of ten thousands of people who have set themselves against me all around. (vv. 1-6)

Whenever I read what that Psalm says about lying down and sleeping in safety, it always reminds me of the Apostle Peter. In the early days of the Church, he was imprisoned for preaching about Jesus and sentenced to die. The night before he was to be executed, he slept so soundly in jail that when the angel of God came to deliver him, he had to hit Peter to wake him up. Don't you love it? Peter wasn't pacing his jail cell in fear. He was sleeping, surrounded by God's peace and protection.

Jesus said we can do the same thing! He said that even though we live in the last days when men's hearts are "failing them from fear and the expectation of those things which are coming on the earth" (Luke 21:26), we don't have to be afraid. We can just keep living by faith, hedged roundabout and guarded by the protective power of God. We can sleep soundly knowing that He's not wringing His hands and worrying about us. On the contrary, as Psalm 32 says, He's singing songs of deliverance over us!

I think we ought to join Him, don't you?

I think we should just have a sing-along with Jesus and come into agreement with Him and His Word. That's what Paul and Silas did, and it certainly worked well for them. When they were locked up in stocks in the jail at Philippi, they prayed and sang praises unto God so loudly that the other prisoners heard them. "And suddenly there was a great earthquake, so that the foundations of the prison were shaken: and immediately all the doors were opened, and every one's bands were loosed" (Acts 16:26).

"Yeah, but Paul and Silas were apostles!" you might say. "They qualified for that kind of big-time protection."

If you're a born again believer, you do too. Apostle or not, you qualify as the protected, the delivered, the whole, the healed, and the restored. Even if you've sinned and made some major mistakes, God isn't holding sin against you. He'll do whatever it takes to protect you. When you respond to Him according to faith, He'll respond to you according to grace—and His grace is always more than enough. It always brings enough of God's power on the scene to deliver you.

First John 5 in *The Message Bible* puts it like this: "Every God-begotten person conquers the world's ways. The conquering power that brings the world to its knees is our faith...The God-begotten are also the God-protected. The evil one can't lay a hand on them" (vv. 4, 18).

That's the bottom line right there. When you're living by faith in the place of grace, the Evil One can't lay a hand on you. He'll try. He'll trespass and take advantage of you if you don't know how to stand on the Word and resist him. He'll put pressure on you and send people to tell you that God isn't going to deliver you this time. But those people, well-meaning as they might be, aren't saying what the Bible says.

The Bible says you're the God-protected. In every situation. All the time.

But you have to make the choice. To enjoy the benefits of God's place of protection, you have to corral your thinking. You have to remind yourself every day that God is the One who surrounds, protects, and delivers you.

So make the right choice today and every day. Sing along with your heavenly Father and say, as Psalm 91:1 does: "I'm living in the secret place of the Most High God and hiding under the shadow of the Almighty. He's my refuge and my fortress."

Choose to dwell continually by faith in the place of grace where Satan can't lay a hand on you.

12

SHOUT GRACE TO IT!

For you know the grace of our Lord Jesus Christ, that though He was rich, yet for your sakes He became poor, that you through His poverty might become rich.

2 Corinthians 8:9

Over the years, ministering in various churches around the world, I've found that preaching about finances can be risky business. The very mention of the subject seems to make some Christians cranky. On occasion, a few people get so offended at me for bringing it up that they come to me after the service and complain. "Man, for guys like you it's always about the money!" they say.

They're mistaken, of course.

It's not all about the money.

But when it comes to walking in the fullness of God's grace, money is definitely part of the package. We need it to complete the mission God has called us, as believers, to carry out in these last days. We need it to help spread the Gospel to all nations and live the abundant life Jesus has planned for us. We need it in order to be blessed and be a blessing to others.

So even if it makes a few people cranky (not people like you, of course, but other less spiritual people), money is worth talking about. It's a vital part of advancing God's kingdom on earth. To do our part, we need it in abundance. And we don't want to have to get it by bowing down to the ungodly system of this world. We want to find out what the Bible says about how to get prosperity God's way.

Does God really have a way to get money to me? you might wonder.

Yes, He does.

He actually has a plan to prosper you. He has a grace for prosperity. As Second Corinthians 9:8 says, "God is able to make all grace abound toward you, that you, always having all sufficiency in all things, may have an abundance for every good work."

When you receive grace in the area of finances, it empowers you to prosper to an extent you couldn't on your own. Grace supplies you with direction and provides you with ideas that can bring you supernatural increase. It enables you to excel economically so that you experience the fulfillment of the promise given to God's people in Deuteronomy 28:12:

The LORD will open to you His good treasure, the heavens, to give the rain to your land in its season, and to bless all the work of your hand.

The word *treasure* in Hebrew refers to a treasury. It speaks of the unlimited supply in God's heavenly storehouse. That storehouse contains more than we could ever ask for or imagine, and it's open to every one of us as God's children. Once we know how to tap into its resources, we can come out from under the financial pressures and limitations of this fallen world's system. We can gain access to avenues of divine prosperity that make it possible for us to draw on the riches of Heaven while we're still here on earth.

That's really God's economic plan for us. He's given us the key to His heavenly treasury and deposited within us the spirit to prosper so that anytime we choose to embrace it, we can rise up and walk in it.

"But Dennis," you might say, "wouldn't you agree there's a lot more to prospering than just having money?"

Absolutely.

I've seen numbers of people who were financially rich and yet their lives were filled with problems money couldn't solve. I've also known people who didn't have a penny in the bank and yet in other ways they were very rich. But as believers, we aren't limited to just those two options. We don't have to choose either one kind of prosperity or the other. No, according to First Timothy 6:17, "[God] gives us richly all things to enjoy"!

Think about that for a moment. *God gives... all things...to enjoy.*

Nobody *enjoys* poverty. It's not something God gives. It's the devil's invention. It's part of the curse that came into the world through sin, and it's one of the things Jesus came to redeem us from. As He said in Luke 4:18 (CEB), He came to "preach good news to the poor." He came to tell us we don't have to be poor anymore!

Sadly, however, religious tradition has taught just the opposite. It's promoted the idea that poverty is sometimes a good thing; that God uses it to make people more holy. Talk about a ridiculous idea! Financial lack never made anybody more holy. It tends to do just the opposite. It pushes people toward selfishness.

As many of us have discovered from experience, if we don't have enough to pay our bills and put food on the table, we don't tend to focus on how we can help solve somebody else's problems. We're focused on ourselves! Instead of thinking about how we can meet the needs of others, we're thinking about how we can get what we need.

That's not God's plan for us! He established a way for us to step out of poverty into a lifestyle of financial victory that moves us out of selfishness and into selflessness. He wants us to tap into His prospering grace so that instead of focusing on what we can get, we're free to focus on what we can give.

GOD'S SOLUTION TO POVERTY

If you want to see some people who were truly free to give, read in Second Corinthians 8 about the Macedonian believers. They were amazing! They had such a tremendous revelation of God's grace for prosperity that, at a time when they were facing a severe financial challenge themselves, they insisted on giving a major offering to the Christians in famine-stricken Jerusalem. Their generosity so inspired the Apostle Paul that in his letter to the Corinthians, He wrote:

> Moreover, brethren, we make known to you the grace of God bestowed on the churches of Macedonia: that in a great trial of affliction the abundance of their joy and their deep poverty abounded in the riches of their liberality. For I bear witness that according to their ability, yes, and beyond their ability, they were freely willing, imploring us with much urgency that we would receive the gift and the fellowship of the ministering to the saints. And not only as we had hoped, but they first gave themselves to the Lord, and then to us by the will of God. So we urged Titus, that as he had begun, so he would also complete this grace in you as well. But as you abound in everything; in faith, in speech, in knowledge, in all diligence, and in your love for us; see that you abound in this grace also. (vv. 1-7)

The first few verses in that passage always make me chuckle. I think they contain the oddest combination of phrases I've ever seen in a single sentence. To me, concepts like *great affliction* and *abundance of joy* just don't seem to go together. Neither do *deep poverty* and *riches of liberality* (a.k.a. big giving). Yet those are the terms Paul uses to describe the keys to God's prospering grace that the believers in Macedonia had discovered.

Right in the midst of a serious financial trial, they'd found that they could respond in a way that resulted in joy. They'd discovered that instead of caving in to the pressure and letting it drive them into selfishness, they could rise above it by giving. First, they could give themselves to God; and second, they could give eagerly to help meet the needs of other people.

The Macedonian Christians understood that this system of giving and receiving is God's solution to poverty—and they were thrilled about it! They believed Jesus meant it when He said in Luke 6:38, "Give, and it will be given to you: good measure, pressed down, shaken together, and running over..." So in their time of need they insisted on giving.

As Paul put it, "They begged us again and again for the privilege of sharing in the gift" (2 Corinthians 8:4, NLT).

From a natural perspective that sounds backwards doesn't it? When people are under financial pressure, they usually want money coming to them, not going from them. But that's not how we, as believers, are supposed to think. We're supposed to believe the Bible, and it says if we're in economic trouble or if we want to increase financially, we're to do what the Macedonian believers did. We're to get our priorities straight by giving ourselves to God and giving into His kingdom as He directs us.

We're not supposed to give just every once in a while, either. According to Paul, we're to *abound* in this grace!

Why was Paul so emphatic about this?

Because he knew that God doesn't want His people just living according to the world's financial status quo. He's looking to raise us up to a higher level. To unhook us from the spirit of lack and lift us into the place of supernatural prosperity. To teach us to handle money His way so that He can give us all that we could possibly use!

One of the churches in Macedonia that caught sight of this was the church at Philippi. They so appreciated the benefits of God's prospering grace that they not only participated in the offering for the believers in Jerusalem, they partnered financially with Paul's ministry. As he said in the letter he wrote them:

> ...no church shared with me concerning giving and receiving but you only. For even in Thessalonica you sent aid once and again for my necessities. Not that I seek the gift, but I seek the fruit that abounds

to your account. Indeed I have all and abound. I am full, having received from Epaphroditus the things sent from you, a sweet-smelling aroma, an acceptable sacrifice, well pleasing to God. And my God shall supply all your need according to His riches in glory by Christ Jesus. (Philippians 4:14-19)

Notice Paul makes it clear there that it wasn't all about the money for him. It was about the fruit that was going to abound in the lives of the Philippian believers. It was about the eternal rewards they would receive. It was about God meeting all their needs according to His riches in glory. It was also about the special way their giving would connect them to Paul's ministry. Their giving qualified them to share in the anointing that was upon him. "Because you have been my partners in spreading the Good News about Christ..." Paul said, "you all are partakers of my grace" (Philippians 1:5, 7, NLT, NKJV).

NOT JUST "FILTHY LUCRE"

The spiritual power of financial partnership is something Vikki and I found out about early in our walk with the Lord. So in 1973 when we got married, even though we'd just been born again a couple of years, there was never a question about whether or not we were going to give tithes and offerings. It was a settled issue. Because we knew our giving honored God and supernaturally connected us to the ministries in His kingdom, we immediately made it a part of our lives together.

As a result, when God joined us to the first church we attended, we did more than just put our names on the roll and show up on Sunday morning to hear what the pastor had to say. We became partners with that church and took financial responsibility.

What's more, we were excited about it!

Why were we excited?

Because partnership opens the door to a lot of benefits! Taking on responsibility gives us the right to reap rewards. As believers, when we give to a ministry of God, we become shareholders in it, so to speak. We become partakers of the grace that's upon that ministry.

In addition, as human beings, our heart follows our money, so when we give to God's work our passion for it increases. We don't have to ask somebody to pray for us to become more mission-minded. If we want to have more of a heart for missions, all we have to do is get out our checkbook, write out a check, and send it to a missionary. Once we're involved financially with that missionary, our heart will get involved too. Pretty soon we'll be reading about what he's doing out there on the mission field. We'll be praying for him, saying, "Oh, Lord, help him! Give him favor and power to win souls!"

This proves that money in itself is not a dirty thing. It's not just filthy lucre. Although it can be filthy if pursued for the wrong motives and used for the wrong purposes, it can also be clean and godly when used for good.

Money doesn't have a spirit of its own. It takes on the spirit of whoever is handling it. The same dollars exchanged in a drug deal last night can feed a poor family next week. The same finances that fueled the work of the devil last month can help finance the preaching of the Gospel this month. It all depends on whose hands the money ends up in.

"But Dennis, doesn't the Bible say that money is the root of all evil?"

No, it doesn't. It says "the *love* of money is the root of all evil" (1 Timothy 6:10).

Loving money and having money are two different things. In every big city in the world there are criminals who are flat broke yet they're so in love with money they'll kill you for $25. In those same cities there are people who have plenty of money and are so in love with God and with people that they're giving it away right and left. For the first group, money is a root of evil. For the second group, it's something spiritual and holy that actually "increases the fruit of their righteousness" (2 Corinthians 9:10).

One story in the Bible that demonstrates just how spiritual money can be is the story of Cornelius. He was a wealthy centurion in the Roman army, who lived in a city not far from Jerusalem during the days of the early church. The Bible describes him as "a devout man...who feared God with all his household, who gave alms generously to the people, and prayed to God always" (Acts 10:2). As a Gentile, Cornelius didn't hear the Gospel when it was first preached by the apostles after Jesus' resurrection, so he didn't know anything about it. But he was hungry to know God, and one day as he was praying and seeking more spiritual light, he had a life-changing experience.

> ...he saw clearly in a vision an angel of God coming in and saying to him, "Cornelius!" And when he observed him, he was afraid, and said, "What is it, lord?" So he said to him, Your prayers and your alms have come up for a memorial before God. Now send men to Joppa, and send for Simon whose surname is Peter...He will tell you what you must do. (vv. 3-6)

Notice the way the angel worded that statement. He didn't say, as we might expect, that it was just Cornelius's prayers that had gotten God's attention. He said Cornelius's giving had also come up before God. That's an amazing thought, isn't it? Most people don't even consider the possibility that sowing financially into the work of God and the lives of His people can actually produce spiritual blessings in their life. Yet in this instance that's exactly what happened.

Cornelius's giving, along with his prayers, opened the door to the spiritual answers he was seeking. The finances he invested in God's kingdom helped pave the way for him to be visited by an angel, hear the Gospel from Peter, and become one of the first Gentiles ever to be born again.

What does that say to us, as believers, today?

It says there's a spiritual side to money! When we plant it into the work of God, although it physically leaves our current situation, it remains part of our life. It becomes spiritual seed for our future. It comes up before God as a memorial; He multiplies it, and sends it back to us in whatever form we need.

Think again about what Jesus said in Luke 6:38. "Give, and it will be given to you: good measure, pressed down, shaken together, and running over will be put into your bosom." As believers, we profess to believe that, but sometimes we hesitate to act on it because we're meditating more on running out than on running over. Worried that we're not going to have enough, we wonder, *If I give to somebody else, it will help them…but what will happen to me?*

Jesus has already told us what will happen!

We'll reap a harvest of multiplied blessing in our lives. Instead of coming up short, we'll receive an overflow of God's goodness—spiritually and financially. We'll experience for ourselves the fulfillment of the promise the Apostle Paul made to his ministry partners in Philippians 4:19:

My God shall supply all your need according to His riches in glory by Christ Jesus.

THE QUESTION WE HAVE TO ANSWER

"But Philippians 4:19 doesn't specifically mention the word prosperity," somebody might argue. "It just promises God will supply our needs."

That's true. So here's the question we need to answer: what exactly are our needs?

"Well, we need a house to live in."

No, we don't. People all over the world live without houses. So that can't possibly be a need.

"Okay, then, we need clothes to wear."

Not really. Most all of us already have clothes hanging in our closet. So that need is already met.

"Oh. How about food, then? We definitely need food, don't we?"

Yes, but not much. Millions of people around the world live on a handful of rice and a few bites of meat a day. So apparently that's all the food we really need.

In light of those facts, it's obvious Philippians 4:19 isn't just promising us that God will supply us with what we need to survive. It's not just saying we can trust Him to give us a cardboard box to live in, a few flimsy rags to wear, and just enough food to keep us from starving to death. That's not what it means to have all our needs supplied according to God's riches in glory.

"God's riches in glory" refers to wealth beyond most people's imagination! It includes everything we need to enjoy our lives, be a blessing to others, and finish everything God has called us to do.

It can take a lot of money to finish everything God has called us to do!

I found that out a couple of years after I started my ministry. Having stepped out to obey God, in 1981 I was confronted with the biggest financial need I'd ever faced. I went to Him about it in prayer, hoping He'd tell me how He was going to bring in the income I needed. But instead He gave me another expensive assignment.

He said, "Son, I want you to go to Sydney, Australia, and attend the conference Kenneth Copeland is hosting there."

It was not what I wanted to hear. At that point in my life, every dollar was a big deal, and I'd have to spend a lot of dollars to travel from Texas to Australia. I'd have to buy airline tickets. I'd have to pay to stay in a hotel for five or six days. I'd have to buy meals. While the cash register in my head rang up the expenses, the Holy Spirit reminded me that regardless of the cost I really had only two choices. I could either say, "Yes," to the Lord and do what He'd told me to do, or say,

"No," and disobey Him. Since, for me, the latter was not an option, I said, "All right, Lord, I'll go."

I talked to Vikki about it, and she supported the decision. Although we didn't have the money for her to go with me, she agreed I should make the trip. So I made the plans, bought the ticket, and found a place to stay while I was in Sydney.

On the flight there, the Lord spoke to my heart. "This is a scouting trip for your ministry," He said. "I'll introduce you to a man who will open the door for you to minister in the nation of Australia for years to come."

Back at home, Vikki was praying and believing God to supply all our needs according to His riches in glory. On Sunday she went to the church we'd recently begun attending. During the service, the pastor stopped right in the middle of his sermon and pointed her out to the congregation. "This is Vikki Burke, folks," he said. "Her husband travels all over the place preaching the Gospel, so he's somewhere else today. Where is he, Vikki?"

"Well, he's in Australia right now," she said.

"Australia!" he exclaimed. "That's the other side of the world! We're going to receive an offering and give it all to Dennis Burke Ministries today so we can sow into what he's doing there."

The offering that Sunday morning turned out to be big enough to pay all the bills for my entire trip! What's more, just as the Lord promised, in

Australia I met someone who wound up being a major blessing in my ministry. That's what it looks like when God meets all our needs according to His riches in glory!

SOWING COMES FIRST

"But Dennis, everybody doesn't have those kinds of experiences!"

I know it. But that's not because God doesn't want them to. He wants all of us to connect with His prospering grace. He wants all of us to reap the financial benefits that belong to us as His children. But to do so, we must connect with the spiritual system He set up. To reap, we first have to sow.

As the Bible says:

- He who sows sparingly will also reap sparingly, and he who sows bountifully will also reap bountifully. So let each one give as he purposes in his heart, not grudgingly or of necessity; for God loves a cheerful giver (2 Corinthians 9:6-7).

- Do not be deceived, God is not mocked; for whatever a man sows, that he will also reap. For he who sows to his flesh will of the flesh reap corruption, but he who sows to the Spirit will of the Spirit reap everlasting life. And let us not grow weary while doing good, for in due season we shall reap if we do not lose heart (Galatians 6:7-9).

A few years ago the Lord gave me a spiritual picture that gave me fresh insight into those verses. I'd been meditating on the concept of reaping when, with the eyes of my heart, I saw myself in a large field, sowing seed by hand into tilled ground. In the vision, I was so focused on sowing the seed that I mostly kept my head down, looking at the soil, intent on what I was doing. But every once in a while, I'd stop and look back at the rows I had planted. I'd notice how straight they were and felt very good about that.

Eventually, I finished sowing the entire field. As I stood there surveying it, I started noticing other fields all around me stretching as far as I could see. Unlike the field I had just planted where the seed had just been put in the ground, in the surrounding fields I could see a great harvest ready to be reaped.

While I was looking at that harvest, John 4:38 flashed across my mind. "I sent you to reap that for which you have not labored; others have labored, and you have entered into their labors." Instantly, I knew by the Holy Spirit that the harvest in all those adjoining fields was mine. It didn't belong to somebody else. It belonged to me. I had access to it because of what I had just sown.

I'll never forget how clearly I saw it at that moment. This is what happens when we do what God tells us to do about sowing and we tap into His financial grace! His grace gives us access to supernatural harvest in our lives. It enables us to prosper far beyond our own natural ability. It empowers us to increase, not according to what we've done, but according to what Jesus has done.

Jesus is the One whose labors we're entering into. He's the One who provides for us "grace upon grace" (John 1:16, NASB). He's the Source of our every success.

It's Jesus who gives us the wisdom to know which piece of property to buy and which one to leave alone; what client to accept and what client to turn down; what job to take or what business to start. It's Jesus who enables us to avoid financial pitfalls and empowers us to prosper according to God's riches in glory. We're able to do it all because of Him and because of the Spirit of grace He imparts to us every single day.

There's a passage in the Old Testament Book of Zechariah that illustrates beautifully this ongoing work of grace in our lives. It's about a man named Zerubbabel who was called by God to help rebuild the Jewish Temple. From a human perspective, the task seemed impossible, the obstacles as big as a mountain. But as Zerubbabel stood wondering one day how he could ever finish his divine mission, he got a word from a prophet of God that changed everything:

> This is the word of the LORD to Zerubbabel: "Not by might nor by power, but by My Spirit," says the LORD of hosts. "Who are you, O great mountain? Before Zerubbabel you shall become a plain! And he

shall bring forth the capstone with shouts of Grace, grace to it! (Zechariah 4:6-7)

This is how you and I, as believers, are going fulfill the call of God in these last days. This is how we, as the Church, are going to walk in the spirit of Elijah, do the impossible, and prepare this world for the second coming of the Lord. We're going to do it the way God told Zerubbabel to do it—not by our might nor by our power, but by the Spirit of Almighty God! We're going to complete every assignment God has given us, with shouts of faith that will echo throughout eternity, "Grace! Grace to it!"

Dr. Dennis Burke is internationally known as a Bible teacher and author. Since 1979, Dennis has helped thousands discover how to live a victorious life through faith in God's Word. Dennis has been the keynote speaker in churches, conventions, and seminars around the world.

Dennis and his wife, Vikki, are co-founders of Dennis Burke Ministries in Arlington, Texas. They have one married daughter, Jessica Shook. In 2003, Dennis earned his Doctorate in Theology from Life Christian University, Tampa, Florida.

They have authored numerous bestselling books such as *How to Meditate God's Word* and *The Satisfied Life* and Vikki's popular titles, *Some Days You Dance* and *Destiny Held Hostage.*

BOOKS BY DENNIS BURKE

Dreams Really Do Come True—
It Can Happen to You!
Develop a Winning Attitude
Breaking Financial Barriers
You Can Conquer Life's Conflicts
Grace: Power Beyond Your Ability
* How to Meditate God's Word
Knowing God Intimately
The Satisfied Life

* Available in Spanish

AUDIO MESSAGES BY DENNIS BURKE

How to Redefine Your Life
Falling Into Greatness
The Believer's Rightful Place
Secrets to Beat Any Trial
Standing in the Place of Grace

Start your day, armed with *the* Truth.

So many will begin their mornings tuning in to TV news, or fill the quiet with the empty banter of early morning secular talk shows. We all know starting off right can prepare us for victory. Why not fuel up with strength-boosting encouragement and insights from God's Word?

Following are just a few testimonies from the growing number of believers who have chosen to brighten their mornings with the light of God's Word through the DBM *Enriching Life Daily* devotional emails:

"Thank you for saying yes to the Lord and following after His heart. Your daily inspirationals are so anointed… clear, precise and Life giving. You and Dennis follow the heart beat of the Lord. Jesus continue to bless all you put your hand to and increase your circle of influence for His Kingdom. Much love in Him…"

"Thank you for this email, it was exactly what I needed today. God bless you for the work you are doing in extending God's kingdom."

"Thank you for your daily emails…they are such a blessing to me and help me with my walk with God. I look forward to them everyday and they encourage me in God's Word daily! I am so thankful for God bringing you into my life through my church. You are awesome and thank you so so much! Blessing to you both…"

testimonies

Try *Enriching Life Daily* with Vikki Burke!
DennisBurkeMinistries.org

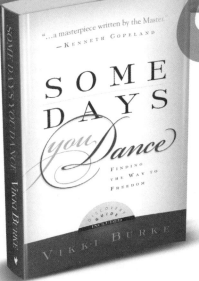

Insights
at home or on the go

Now you can choose to enjoy each issue of Dennis Burke Ministries *Insights* magazine online—or in print. If you have not yet signed up to receive your copy of *Insights* delivered to your door, follow this link for a free subscription:

dennisburkeministries.org/**insights-magazine.html**

Follow this link to begin reading immediately on your computer or mobile device:

http://dennisburkeministries.org/**insights_welcome.html**